new urban giants

© 2008 White Star S.p.A.
Via Candido Sassone, 22/24
13100 Vercelli, Italy
www.whitestar.it

ISBN 978-88-544-0332-1

Reprint:
1 2 3 4 5 6   12 11 10 09 08

Color separation: CTM, Turin
Printed in Indonesia

new urban giants
the ultimate skyscrapers

edited by
Antonino Terranova

text by
Gianpaola Spirito
Antonino Terranova

WHITE STAR PUBLISHERS

EDITED BY

ANTONINO TERRANOVA

TEXT

GIANPAOLA SPIRITO
ANTONINO TERRANOVA

Editorial project

VALERIA MANFERTO DE FABIANIS

Editorial coordination

FEDERICA ROMAGNOLI

Graphic design

CLARA ZANOTTI

Graphic layout

MARIA CUCCHI

5 ■ The 12-inch space between the two glass skins of the façade of the Deutsche Post headquarters in Bonn, designed by architects Murphy/Jahn, houses an installation by French artist Yann Kersalé: at night the building is illuminated in shades of red, blue or yellow, changing its appearance with its color.

7 ■ The Tour EDF by Henry N. Cobb is situated in Paris' La Défense district. Its volume, enclosed in a reflective glass skin with bronze-colored steel bands, creates a convex façade at the point where it intersects the *Axe historique* with which La Défense is aligned.

CONTENTS

introduction

"The face of the earth would be much altered if brick architecture were ousted everywhere by glass architecture. It would be as if the earth were adorned with sparkling jewels and enamels. Such glory is unimaginable. All over the world it would be as splendid as in the gardens of the *Arabian Nights*. We should then have a paradise on earth, and no need to watch in longing expectation for the paradise in heaven." Paul Scheerbart (1863–1915) was in favor of a sort of utopian love, promoting the reproduction of nature instead of reproduction per se, as illustrated by his laudatory raptures on glass cited above.

This idealist vision belongs to the same genre as the sketches and writings of Bruno Taut (1880–1938), such as *The City Crown* or *The Dissolution of the Cities* (1920). These striking and highly evocative examples conjure up images of a humanity able to live directly in an open land, with marvelous landscapes and metaphorical rather than constructional architecture, which paraphrases nature's animal, vegetable and mineral kingdoms. The same theme recurs in the drawings of Hermann Finsterlin (1887–1973), Rudolf Steiner (1861–1925), Hans Scharoun (1893–1972) and Antoni Gaudí (1852–1926), who also designed a New York skyscraper hotel (Hotel Attraction). A dramatic sculptural, vitalist or expressionist dimension can also be found in the works of delineator Hugh Ferriss (1889–1962), who illustrated the *Regional Plan of New York and its Environs*, in the drawings of his *Imaginary Metropolis;* in the paintings of Georgia O'Keeffe (1887–1986); and in the designs of skyscrapers with curved and triangular plans by Ludwig Mies van der Rohe (1886–1969) built before the Seagram Building, the prototype of the "glass box," which is both an emblem of rationalism and imbued with an exciting uniqueness.

In many of what we could define the "new giants" – skyscrapers with futuristic forms that are gradually colonizing all the world's major cities – there appears to be a dreamy vitalism that is both oneiric and synthetic. Sail-shaped or conical giants are no longer even considered kitsch: they are an excursus from the world of architectural discipline, a digression from the professional mediation of construction, at the hands of the most uninhibited international stars of architecture and the leading engineering firms, who put their sophisticated technology at the service of the most outlandish reveries.

Over a century from their birth and early diffusion, skyscrapers are among the most characteristic building types of the Modern style. They were based on what was the completely new concept of stacking multiple stories and used mass-produced panels typical of the Industrial age, although they actually summoned up archetypes such as the palace, the tower and the belfry (but also the mountain, the canyon, the ravine and the stalactite), which they eccentrically combined with futuristic science-fiction prototypes (Flash Gordon and the Superheroes, Moebius and Enki Bilal). In this respect they are practically contemporary with cinema, the seventh art or tenth muse, and the multimedia works that currently represent its evolution but also its distortion. It is thus not surprising that skyscrapers naturally belong to what has been defined as the society of images, entertainment, communication and the mass avant-garde. Skyscrapers have always played an important role in the spheres of cinema and multimedia from the time of their proto-modern origins. And indeed, cinema has celebrated its centenary with a myriad of remakes and sequels, tracing the customs and legends of its past, as in the case of the latest *King Kong* movies.

The 1950s marked a historic stage in the development of the skyscraper, with the appearance of the rectangular metal, glass and concrete blocks of the Seagram Building and the United Nations Headquarters, designed respectively by Mies van der Rohe and Le Corbusier. These gleaming boxes propose anti-decorative cleanliness, seriality, modularity and the precision of the overall design and its details as positive values in themselves, combined with the high density that allows the concentration of inhabitants, offices and flows with what was known as a strong "urban effect." The "boxes" multiplied indefinitely throughout the world's metropolises, colonizing them with clusters of downtown buildings, where tens of thousands of people are crowded into a few central blocks, connected with service, nodal and intermodal infrastructures, as exemplified by the World Trade Center and the subway stations and pedestrian areas that were located beneath it and around it. The forms of the buildings had changed more than their functional urban role, and the outsized dimensions of the Twin Towers, which appear even more impressive in the void left on the Manhattan skyline and at Ground Zero, belonged to the new formalism of the Mannerist Modern style. When the towers were destroyed in the terrorist attack, these values had long been transformed into disvalues, symbols of standardization, boredom and the regimentation of the prevailing technocratic technicism. With advent of Postmodernism, the Modernist ideologies of precision and sincerity or tectonic and functional transparency, and the actual freedom afforded to architecture by technical innovations (structural skeletons, efficient autonomous systems, increasing relative independence of the outer shell and the fluid inner spaces) were playfully underscored. There was thus a sudden reemergence of the symbolic or allegorical themes of superrational imagery bordering on the architectural, which skyscrapers recall by nature.

During this period new analyses, with new interpretative categories, were required, resulting in a series of publications, including Rem Koolhaas' *Delirious New York* (1978) and Frederic Jameson's *Postmodernism: The Cultural Logic of*

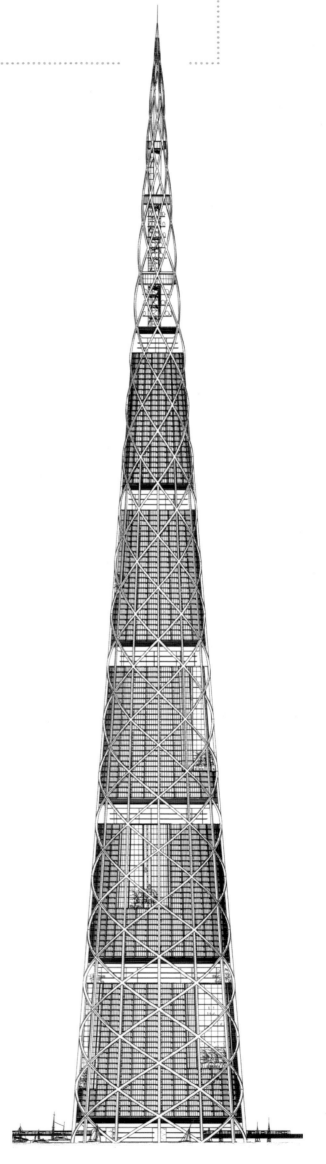

10 ■ **Study for the Nara Tower (Tokyo),**
Ken Yeang, 1994.

Late Capitalism (1984). The latter compares the form of the typical skyscraper with the monolith in *2001: A Space Odyssey*, which marked the evolutionary stages in the history of mankind, and investigates its loss of "depth" and ambiguous enigmatic nature following the "breakdown of the relationship between signifiers." Jameson also draws on John Portman's Bonaventure Hotel in Los Angeles (1977) to illustrate the new spatiality and figurativeness of the city's architecture, which he interprets as signs of a radical break or *coupure* with the forms of the object (architectural) that seems to transcend the evolution of the subject (human), which has difficulty in explaining its own most bizarre or extreme work. New definitions for skyscrapers also emerged, such as "skyprick" for exaggeratedly tall towers and "skycities" for clusters that tend to alter and three-dimensionalize the entire urban fabric.

Today's giants seem to combine glimpses of elements drawn from the genres of science fiction or fantasy – a sort of cross between *2001: A Space Odyssey, Blade Runner, Batman* and *Superman* – with the utopian designs of the radical architects of the 1960s, such as Archigram and the Metabolists, Hollein and Sacripanti, Kahn and Nouvel. The utopia of humanity freed from the bonds of urban architecture produced a kind of fantasy architecture akin to fantasy literature and movies. However, it entails the same risk as the flat sky of the lands of wonders and treasures inhabited by unicorns, winged horses and flying carpets among minarets and gilded domes, i.e., that everything eventually looks the same, becoming cloying and boring.

These new giants are currently working a great transformation of the Earth's crust, both by characterizing the new – very diverse and unexpected – centers of the territories, and by creating new images of cities that can be globally marketed as

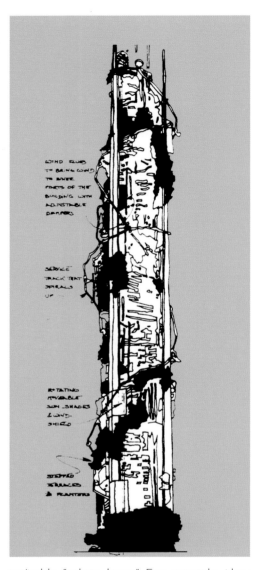

veritable "urban logos." For example, they are increasingly frequently used to brand the websites of the great cities competing for world leadership in the fields of finance, tourism and entertainment. Nonetheless, several emphatic veins of formalism persist. One of the ways that they manage do so is by multiplying the examples of historical quotation, a trend born with Postmodernism around 1980, that appears almost as a paradoxical and extremely decorative and evocative new International Style (reminiscent of the Art Deco style of the Empire State Building and Chrysler Building, for example). Its stylistic features have a declared flavor of plastic and artificiality created with synthetic materials, and employ planetary pastiches in a cynical language standardized in the eccentric framework of make-believe. There are also numerous examples of forms that evoke eco-efficiency, carving terraces out of outer sur-

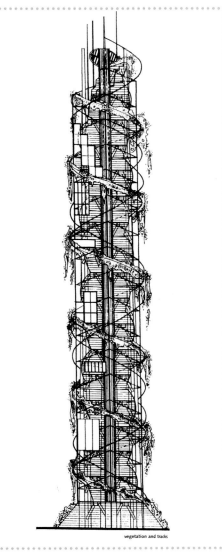

vegetation and tracks

faces characterized by closely woven textures that regulate the building's temperature, ventilation and illumination through exchange between the inside and outside, sometimes even simulating vitalistic organic or post-organic morphologes, like those of genetically modified organisms. Finally, a strange hybridization of deconstructionist postures and post-organic suppleness produces a jumble of towers – structures as well as simply façades – that are bent and twisted, kinked or leaning, and resemble crystal formations, vegetables or animals.

The prime aim of the most futuristic new giants is to reach even dizzier heights, but they also take the form of multiform and multipurpose city-building complexes, served by infrastructures in ways that have already been partially experimented. They are situated in affectedly artificial urban settings, such as groups of manmade islands or bays. Finally, their technological structures

and features combine criteria of eco-efficiency with emphatic high-tech virtuoso feats. Today there are no radical technological innovations comparable to the early ones, such as elevators, steel and glass frames and air-conditioning. Instead a series of refinements have taken the limit of the possible to extremes, for increased height is accompanied by a prevalence of horizontal loads, changing the architectural morphology of structures, while the quest for eco-efficiency and energy savings has become the prime environmental factor in design.

However, the giants are not simply ever taller or larger structures, but also increasingly polymorphous and difficult to interpret. They have swelled the ranks of the "metropolitan monsters," i.e., those structures without the form of buildings, which are designed to stand out from the ordinary urban fabric of their habitat to amaze onlookers with their wonderful and surprising appearance. In short, the new giants belong to the category of "metropolitan monsters" in the peculiar sense of buildings with an immoderate ambition to inhabit the sky, or "sculpt the skies." The very nature of these new giants places them in the world of the monsters, for they have abandoned the aspects of rationality that had been considered appropriate for skyscrapers ever since the term was coined by Louis Sullivan (1856–1924) – i.e., the maximum expression of the concept of verticality – and instead enjoy the freedom allowed by technological progress, despite the ideas of coherent organic unity propounded by the Modernist movement. They belong to the world of the "monsters" from the outset, not only because of their immense height, but also due to the basic notion of "quantity," a monstrously concentrated amount of cubic feet, infrastructures and services, with loads and stress multiplied in a hyperbolic combination of human inhabitants, functional and symbolic flows.

The new giants also establish new relations between architecture, art (no longer merely visual, and in particular the so-called "archisculptures" by the international stars of architecture) and, above all, design, which increasingly proposes itself as the alternative to what was once known as fine arts or the "arts of drawing." Design is no longer simply the industrial design of early modernity, intended as the qualitative improvement of products by the application of mass construction and manufacturing, but has become playful and alluring, and tends to impose its consumption/production/ consumption methods on the traditional methods of architecture and urban architecture. In the contemporary metropolis the cities themselves, or their distinctive districts, present themselves as objects of design, singular objects and logos invested with great semantic significance, which enter the information and communication networks of marketing. The international stars of architecture play a special role in this extreme game, which seems radically devoid of historically established symbolic and cultural values. A disconcerting but emblematic example is the recent case of the United Arab Emirates, whose development appears largely boundless, with Abu Dhabi and Dubai competing to conquer a strongly iconic urban image through the construction of skyscrapers and other striking works of architecture. The resulting cities are difficult to define unless totally removed from the two contemporary models – the European city and the American city.

The urban architecture of the third millennium seems to have gone insane and the outsized, out-of-proportion height of the new giants – now deliberately and atrociously "ungrammatica" – is sufficient to place them at the center of this madness. Is there a method in this madness of ceaselessly eccentric constructions and deconstructions, apparently lacking a coherent

structure like an organic corporeal skeleton; egotistic and competitive in relation to their neighbors and their entire context; indifferent and almost irreverent towards all serious architectural discipline?

In truth, it is not the first time that architecture has departed from the tracks, negating the scholastic application of the Vitruvian trio of *firmitas*, *utilitas* and *venustas*, along with Alberti's concept of *concinnitas*, according to which a house is a small city and a city is a large house. Yet buildings from all eras (such as the colossal temples of Paestum from the 6th century BC; Haghia Sophia in Istanbul dating from AD 532; the 12th-century cathedral of Notre Dame in Paris; Florence cathedral, built between 1296 and 1462; Palazzo Farnese erected in 1552; and the 18th-century Belvedere palace in Vienna), despite being constructions with exceptional features, seem to contain the elements and hierarchical grammar of an architectural code, with a coherent, consistent concept of city around them. Even the giants of the Manhattan tycoons (the Empire State Building, the Chrysler Building and the Rockefeller Center), with their ostentatious eccentric shapes and spires, comply with the rules of an urban fabric with a regular rectangular grid and follow the dictates of uniform zoning regulations and a capitalistic urban and landed administration capable of affording itself special, yet not uncontrolled, exceptions. After all, at a very early stage skyscrapers started to express not only their initial and preliminary verticality, but also a sculptural formalistic vocation that is an end unto itself, or rather unto the pure game of skill, risk, dizziness and mimicry permitted by the unprincipled and almost unwittingly lucid use of technology and its fantastic potential. The striking difficulty of classifying the new giants reveals how they have often been built with the intention of being unclassifiable due to their tireless originality (i.e., their

recognizability is derived from their absolute individuality).

Today the skylines from west to east are punctuated by an array of gleaming figures that are simultaneously always different and always the same, ends unto themselves in their shimmering paleness, deliberately devoid of strong constructive reasons and bearing little relation to habitable building types, as though people lived indifferently in crystals and gherkins, rocky shards and pagodas, black boxes and pinnacles. This emphatic gaiety blooming with captivating forms and attractive lights and colors offers diffusive and perennially charming architecture and happiness, almost as though happiness were not, as the philosopher warns, a constantly ephemeral state for mankind. It is as though people, gathering in their thousands inside the giants, encamped in an urban realm often constituted by masses of millions of beings, were happy to inhabit giant anthills or beehives, in metaphors of very diverse terrestrial landscapes, sorely tried by the metastasis of the urban realm, as if it were not the multitude of humans that build the giants, but rather the giants that were a living race, allowing people to inhabit them in order to feed off them. And it is as though their forms were independent of their inhabitants and were instead chosen by a sort of "superhuman humans" with the power, and perhaps also the divine function, of organizing the land and sculpting the skies.

In both the business and entertainment (or infotainment) capitals of the classic West and the metropolises of the East, the new giants rise around the transition between the millennia and are even more gigantic or bizarre than their predecessors. But their pervasive polymorphous diffusion in the relocation and reconfiguration of the postmodern or contemporary modern habitat is also gigantic, and often also unpredictable and unexpected. Like flags marking

strategic geographical maps, they show the geopolitical and perhaps also cultural shift that had already been announced at the end of the last century, when – before the destruction of New York's Twin Towers – the twin towers of Kuala Lumpur became the tallest building in the world. They multiply in the planetary metropolis with multiple aggregations and dimensions, and thus we find entire residential quarters of tall buildings, central districts with clusters of skyscrapers that have come to symbolize the downtown areas, skylines (often coastal) with distinctive and unmistakable silhouettes, and also, every now and then, skyscrapers as singular objects, rising from the urban fabric like territorial – but primarily communicational – landmarks, contrasting with their surrounding environments. Particularly distinctive are the exuberant forms of the New Easts, which competitively rearrange the traditions of the West until distorting them, separating them out into their historical components, or pushing them in the most extreme futuristic directions to combine technology and eco-efficiency.

The already-old slogan "not so Far East" has been outmoded by the now acknowledged centrality of Oriental, but by no means exotic, universes that have instead surpassed the methods and models of Western development. They are universes where strength, power and vendetta are clearly expressed, without European censorship, on an absolute symbolic primordial level. "China's New DREAMSCAPE" was the cover story of an issue of Time magazine, flanked by a drawing juxtaposing two of the towers of Shanghai's famous skyline (the pagoda-like Jin Mao Building and the Oriental Pearl Tower with its colored spheres) and two of Beijing's "metropolitan monsters" built for the 2008 Olympic Games (Herzog & de Meuron's "Bird Nest" National Stadium and Rem Koolhaas' loop-shaped CCTV Headquarters). The subtitle announced: "The world's most visionary architects are transforming the Middle Kingdom in the greatest building boom ever." That which the entertainment industry intended and built as a playful kitsch reconstruction in the form of the New York-New York Hotel & Casino in Las Vegas, with replicas of the Empire State Building, the Chrysler Building and other iconic skyscrapers plus the Statue of Liberty, is currently being repeated, without any hint of irony – but rather with arrogant assertiveness – by the emergent poles of the New Easts.

The most remarkable towers in Europe, 30 St Mary Axe by Norman Foster and the Agbar Tower by Jean Nouvel, are located respectively in London and Barcelona. Both have a phallic form, apparent in their nicknames (such as "gherkin" or "dildo") and share the aim of dramatically transforming the urban skyline, but the similarities end there. Foster's building, consistent with the city in which it is located and the designer's inclination to present himself as a the jeweler-entrepreneur architect of high-tech, has a wide diagrid structure, which constitutes a sort of gigantic order proportional to the overall dimensions of the building and its presence in the city. At the same time it is pleasantly surprising in relation to the inhabitants of each indivicual story, who are always surrounded by sloping rods and their joints on a scale far beyond the dimensions of man celebrated by the rationalism of the Modernist movement. This aspect is evident in several films featuring 30 St Mary Axe (such as *Match Point* by Woody Allen). The building is situated in the true heart of the City of London, together with the cluster of small- or medium-height towers that originally characterized the area. The tower's strange presence in the urban space is also worthy of note, for its access and circulation areas are open, further emphasizing the gigantic structural diagrid, yet it disappears from sight for

those who look up, seeking in vain its curved top in the sky. Nouvel's tower, on the other hand, appears incoherent in regard to the traditional city and brutally throws its skyline off balance, engaging perhaps only with Gaudi's Sagrada Família and the pinnacle-like forms of the nearby hills. It wittily fits in with Barcelona's strange, surreal imageability – which not only boasts Gaudí, but also Miró and Picasso – marrying its harsh impact on the cityscape with the enjoyable playfulness of its forms. The structural technology is sophisticated but traditional, for Nouvel concentrated his visual technological invention in the skin of his singular object by means of a variable series of screening and lighting systems, and with iridescent color effects that accompany the declared aesthetic intention to dematerialize the construction from the finite to the infinite, until the volume disappears from the gaze in the sky as it curves at its apex.

Are there actually any differences between the "monster" designed by Rem Koolhaas for CCTV in Beijing, Foster and Nouvel's splendid lingams and the thousands of amusing towers that are merely postmodern and historicist masquerades inspired by bell towers and pagodas? Or between the equally numerous towers resulting from the combination of technologies and volumes (as virtuosic as they are inexplicable) and the three towers designed for the redevelopment of Milan's old Fiera complex by Zaha Hadid, Arata Isozaki and Daniel Libeskind, which resemble a demented pack of outsized slabs, straight, bent, contorted, seemingly suspended and curved by the illusory, acrobatic tricks of a funambulist architect? The three Milan skyscrapers, designed by three international stars of architecture, appear as an assembly of heterogeneous hyper-formalisms that illustrate how, by sculptural virtuosity, each form seems truly possible due to technological, constructional and engineering progress.

introduction

Paradoxically, the principle of unity appears to lie in the jarring coexistence of the different and divergent entities. It makes no sense to question the beauty or ugliness of the result: the aim is to surprise – and shock – traditional tastes.

The two towers currently competing for the title of world's tallest building are in Taipei and Dubai and are very different constructions. Taipei 101 follows the new tradition of the pagoda reworked with a kind of telescopic organic form, as though each story had sprouted out of that below, imitating the growth of many exotic plants. However, this tendency to quote from historic buildings is rooted in local monumental forms, with bizarre effects for the Western and Modernist viewer. Burj Dubai, on the other hand appears as an exaggerated form of the ziggurat-type skyscraper, like a hyperbolic representation of the exertion of building with successively smaller blocks until reaching hitherto unimaginable heights for a city that has risen in the desert.

These sensational and irregular metamorphoses, unmediated contrasts without hierarchies or grammatical reasons, have become the paradoxical rule among the Chinese and the ultra-modern Easterners of the Not-So-Far-East: auditoriums in the form of crystals and glaciers, stadiums resembling baskets, towers evoking melting ice or flaming torches, or inspired by bulbous or succulent vegetable forms, wind-eroded rock formations or almost invisible immaterial effects of luminist or diaphanous transparencies.

There is something both old and new in these new giants: a uninhibited naturalness in the use of the most advanced techniques, taken to the far limit of the technological but also to the fantastic extremes of the collective imagination. It involves a paradoxical revival of the most archaic symbols (lingam, corncob, gherkin, mask), albeit within a context in which the "Sign" is prevalently a distinctive mark devoid of any profound meaning whose function or difference is evident only in the infinite semiosis of cosmopolitan relativism. Play is an increasingly present theme, freed from the traditional rules of architectural discipline, uninhibited and desublimated to extremes that may appear uncivilized or barbarian to the canonical and codifying critique. Games of imitation or mimicry, skill or dexterity, vertigo, competition, miniaturization or gigantification, construction, patience or chance: all of these can be identified in the categories defined by Roger Caillois (1913–1978), who distinguished games based on competition, mimicry, risk and dizziness. He also defined two structural categories, separating the rational *ludus* – hence "ludic" – (highly organized games) from *paidea* (freer, less organized games). However, games also take the form of pastimes or can be combined, as in Italo Calvino's *Invisible Cities*, which built on the fantasy/science-fiction themes of the Italian writer's earlier *Cosmicomics*. Dutch historian Johan Huizinga claimed that the category of play is a vital, energetic and neuralgic factor in human life. Games, play and toys: Rem Koolhaas explains the surprising "toy-like" nature of the new giants – particularly the non-Western ones – in sociopolitical terms. His tone has a desperate ring about it, as though he is outclassed by the same "phenomenal phenomenon" that he was the first to recognize, at odds with the cultured categories of modern European architecture. The play of forms, dimensions and materials within habitable space is also an important game – and sometimes a "linguistic game" – for contemporary modern architecture. It becomes increasingly subtle and elegant in contemporary modern buildings, almost like an elite game far removed from the linguistic games of popular culture, whose diffusion has made the

17 ■ The winning project of the international competition for the redevelopment of Fiera Milano
Exhibition Complex, Arata Isozaki, Daniel Libeskind, Zaha Hadid, Pier Paolo Maggiora, 2004

introduction

introduction

18 ▪ Tour Phare in La Défense (Paris),
Morphosis – Thom Mayne, 2006.

transition from the national to the planetary dimension. In the Postmodern period
play assumes its most spontaneous, uninhibited and jocose form, with juggling, acrobatic, spectacular and extreme effects: clim-
bing skyscrapers, leaping between them,
flying and parachuting and hang-gliding
from the top of the tallest towers; or the
classic photographs of Native American
construction workers engaged in feats of
equilibrium on the dizzy heights of construction beams.

It is increasingly rare for the new giants
to belong to the original category of
skyscrapers. Instead, we witness the multi-
plication of examples drawn from the language of play and "natural charmers," pop
giants, historical quotations or simply
symbolic and reminiscent forms. However,
between these two extremes there are
plenty of buildings exemplifying the more so-
ber and refined use of high language, a sort
of softened updated, regularly structured
and technologically sustainable version of
the old much-praised and much-maligned International Style. By contrast, the ultra-
formalistic and hyper-decorative potpourri
features some (admittedly not many) giants
that assume a symbolic value based on subtraction and simplification, almost like a return to the modular and serial box of Mies
van der Rohe's Seagram Building – a model
that was destined to constitute the prototype for the more repetitive standardization of the International Style. It is possible to propose a sort of classification of
the symbolic/linguistic behavior of the new
giants, associated with their dimensions:

1 – The titanic height of the few true "ul-
tra-giant" skyscrapers overrules all linguistic
considerations, constituting a virtuoso feat
verging on the impossible, at what are now
the topographical altitudes of the magic
mountain, with the incredible 1650 feet (503
meters) recently conquered.

2 – Still on the brink of maximum height
as an end unto itself – but obviously aimed
at ensuring visibility and distinctiveness – several new giants assume the forms of the
industrial design objects of mature Moder-
nism: singular objects resembling a cork-
screw rather than a building, or an eco-su-
stainable entity, perhaps with an organic

(vegetable or mineral) metaphorical form, or even that of a gleaming and markedly geometric deluxe technological instrument.

3 – Many medium/tall giants make wide conventional use of the highly recognizable stylistic features of quotationist and historicist Postmodernism (either classicizing or vernacular) combined with the luxurious high-tech style that is often the hallmark of specific hotel chains or commercial brands. Nevertheless, they are generic motifs that have risen to become everyday or commercial conventions, rather than the result of unique or outstanding commissions or designs.

4 – Tall buildings between 300 and 500 ft (c. 90 and 150 m) (thus medium and medium/low) can be found everywhere, but particularly in European cities or the well-established centers of American cities (as in New York, the last "European" city…). They can be placed within the phenomenon of urban restoration and redevelopment that has swept the central districts established between the 19th and 20th centuries. The most diverse formal idioms are featured, but the most frequent component is nonetheless the authorial one expressed by names that are a guarantee of quality, even when they are not those of the international stars of architecture. However, these languages do not spurn brutal recognizability, which they entrust to the shells of highly iconic figures with a strong semiotic or semantic content. The various cities – London, Vienna, Milan, Barcelona – are distinguished by the peculiar positions and arrangements of their new giants.

5 – Entire residential districts are developing alongside the traditional service or financial zones of metropoises – particularly non-Western ones – offering a new and disquieting answer to migration flows, urbanization and the fast-growing need for central managerial functions. They are representative, spectacular and entertaining, but they also satisfy criteria of mass living.

6 -– On a smaller scale, it is possible to identify the designer's intentionality in a building's verticality, which generally refuses to adapt to democratic standardization, i.e., horizontality without any peaks or troughs. Such objects are often innovative and singular in nature, compositional virtuoso feats with the most diverse connotations: spatial and textured effects, metaphorical tricks borrowed from the natural kingdoms (particularly the mineral and vegetable ones), games of subtraction and effects created by precious materials and details extending to immateriality, with the odd return to the past. The same trend can be useful to understand on which "linguistic games" the forms are based and transformed *ad libitum*, endlessly and unrestrainedly, bordering on insignificance.

This brings us back to the Twin Towers and their surprising – and perhaps at the time underestimated – figurative and symbolic inventive power. The Twin or the Double is a prominent symbolic fantasy figure, which has survived the destruction of the World Trade Center in the form of Petronas Towers of Kuala Lumpur, placing the emphasis on the Far East and conquering the height record in a combination of high-tech and historical quotation. However, there is also the figure of the monolith, that of *2001: A Space Odyssey* and that of Mies van der Rohe's Seagram Building, which is the prototype of the standardized and modular box tower, but whose base is subtly decorated with Gothic portals. The composition of the two square monoliths is based on an ambiguous diagonality, a shift that may perhaps be justified, but is nonetheless aesthetically disturbing and confusing because it departs from the regularity of Manhattan's grid without brutality and with spectacular formalistic subtlety. Another element is the tower's ability to appropriate the fantastic dimension of the collective imagination, as

introduction

21 ■ Project for the Tower Verre (New York), Jean Nouvel, 2007.

22-23 ■ 30 St Mary Axe (London), Foster + Partners, 2003.

testified by the leading roles of skyscrapers in motion pictures (particularly in the first three *King Kong* movies). Then there's the theme of dizzy height, which now reappears – or perhaps actually appears for the first time – in the brutal intensity of its absence, maximized by the temporary installation that projected two immaterial vertical columns of light into the sky above Ground Zero. Now the new giants are raising the bar of the challenge even higher, and making it increasingly bizarre. Increasingly defiant of the conventional rules of grammar and construction, they solicit definitions that are more anthropological than aesthetic: euphoric, narcissistic, illusory, obscene, visionary, archisculptural, spectacular-farcical, the mask that does not seem to mask anything, contained in a form without corresponding contents. What destiny awaits us – and for what kind of society? – inside these obligatorily playful scenarios, beneath those pinnacles and phantasmagorical urban lanterns of icons and lights? This hubris of energetic power embodied by toy-like childish forms pertaining to fable or fantasy appears better suited to superheroes and permanently smiling Disney-like anthropomorphic characters than human beings.

Paradoxically struck by his cosmopolitan successes in the Far East and particularly in the Middle East, Rem Koolhaas has probed the disturbing urban essence of the new settlements growing up on the coast and in the desert, no longer in response to the age-old needs of citizens who wish to live in the same place, optimizing their relations, but instead to the rapid, contingent, frantic financial impulses of development. However, they are also underpinned by other types of extreme expressive impulses that have not been satisfied by the earnest serialism of International Style glass boxes and towers. In *Delirious New York* Rem Koolhaas explicitly

states that there is a repressed figurative potential in the "last European city," intended as a crystalline formation or a diagram of real estate values governed by the zoning regulations of the various periods of its history. Indeed the pinnacles and surreal dreams of his disquieting *Delirious New York* convey this unrestrained impulse, straining between the totalitarian doctrine of the superman and democratic mass power, and that which he defines the "final apotheosis of the city." For the city is everywhere, and there is nothing outside the city.

It is also necessary to find a definition, among the derisory negative criticism and the euphoric fascination, for those architects or architecture firms that – sweeping away the morality and moralism of modernity – describe themselves as stars of architecture, just like the stars, divas and goddesses of Hollywood, the glorious and dubious factory of dreams for our fanatical mass childhood. The planetary metropolis continues to ferment with new, inexplicable exaggerated presences, amid growing environmental emergencies. The city itself seems to have gone insane: is it perhaps exercising the theme of fantasy while awaiting the endemic cataclysm of *Blade Runner* or the mysterious apocalypses of *2001: A Space Odyssey*, or an even more futuristic science-fiction scenario? The overly playful game contains happiness and sadness, desire and fear. Something is happening, something that was predicted by Spengler, Le Bon and Ortega y Gasset and the signals of doom announced by borderline historians branded as ultraconservatives, vaticinators and pessimists. We should learn to read them, decipher them and interpret them. As Nietzsche – the prophet of the *Übermensch* on the brink of the chasm – wrote, "One must still have chaos in oneself to be able to give birth to a dancing star."

SHUN HING
SQUARE

[SHENZHEN ■ THE PEOPLE'S REPUBLIC OF CHINA]

The extraordinary development of Shenzhen, which in a short space of time has grown from a poor fishing village into an important business and financial center able to compete with nearby Hong Kong, has required buildings capable of symbolizing this change. It was precisely Shenzhen's proximity to Hong Kong and the wish to assume its role as the region's business and financial hub that prompted the Chinese government to make the city a Special Economic Zone (SEZ).

This induced many investors and professionals to move their businesses to the area, triggering the exponential growth of the village, whose population rose from 30,000 to the current 13 million in the space of a couple of decades. Its rapid development has transformed the entire bank of the Sham Chun River, which marks the boundary with Hong Kong, into an unbroken metropolis that has become known as the Instant City due to the speed with which it has risen and generated the icons that define its distinctive new identity.

As in all Asian metropolises, this identity was expressed in the construction of a series of skyscrapers that compete for the title of the world's highest building, characterized by forms drawn from the local tradition, which has been updated in order to keep it alive.

Shun Hing Square, which was designed in 2 months and built in 40, is a prime example of such structures. At 1260 feet (384 meters), it is one of the world's tallest buildings and stands out clearly on the city's skyline: it is about twice the height of the surrounding towers.

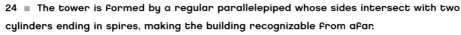

24 ■ The tower is formed by a regular parallelepiped whose sides intersect with two cylinders ending in spires, making the building recognizable from afar.

25 ■ Standing 1260 feet tall, Shun Hing Square dominates the Shenzhen skyline, aspiring to compete with the nearby towers of Hong Kong in terms of height.

26 ■ A detail of the top of the tower, marked by one of the two cylindrical spires topped by an antenna.

27 ■ The complex is formed by the tower, a residential building and a basement housing a shopping mall, which follow the triangular shape of the plot.

← →

The building's original soaring form displays many traditional Chinese elements: the structure features a pair of massive sloping arches that support the sequence of horizontal floors topped by two cylindrical spires and recalls the form of the Chinese character *mei* ("beauty," "beautiful"). The regular design of the cladding, characterized by horizontal bands of windows, is reminiscent of a kung-fu jacket, while the green color of the reflecting glass façade is a symbol of prosperity (it was also used by the Chinese-born architect C. Y. Lee, who now works in Taiwan, for the more recent Taipei 101, in which traditional Chinese symbols are even more evident).

Shun Hing Square stands on a long narrow site, surrounded by a network of roads with heavy traffic.

The complex comprises an underground car park and a base with a five-story shopping mall, from which the tower with offices and a lower residential block rise. Both these blocks are elongated structures and are arranged so that their long façades with the openings are perpendicular, in order to avoid overlooking each other and to benefit from maximum natural lighting. Together they form a triangular shape that points toward an ancient tree.

Each is distinguished by the regular bands of windows on the long sides and the half-cylinders on the short sides; and feature smaller inclined volumes. The various elements are distinguished by the use of different materials: granite for the shopping mall, white tiles with a rotated element clad in red for the apartment block, green reflective glass for the tower, and stone for the intersecting element. The tower has a lozenge plan with a series of steel columns around the perimeter, while the central core is built from reinforced concrete like the shopping arcade. These features permit its slender form, which is nonetheless capable of absorbing the stress produced by typhoons and earthquakes.

LOCATION	PROJECT	HEIGHT	FLOORS	YEAR
SHENZHEN (THE PEOPLE'S REPUBLIC OF CHINA)	K.Y. CHEUNG DESIGN ASSOCIATES	1260 FT 384 M	69	1996

TUNTEX SKY TOWER

[KAOHSIUNG - TAIWAN ◼ THE REPUBLIC OF CHINA]

Many skyscrapers were built at the end of the 1990s, causing the record for the world's highest building to shift from West to East, along with the accompanying economic and financial prestige. They included Cesar Pelli's Petronas Towers in Kuala Lumpur, Skidmore, Owings & Merrill's Jin Mao Building in Shanghai and the Tuntex Sky Tower in Kaohsiung City, by C. Y. Lee. This shift from West to East required its own iconography to impose on the global panorama, and in all three of these cases it drew on forms belonging to the local culture: shapes associated with the vernacular building tradition and symbols or images derived from different contexts that are nonetheless immediately recognizable to the local people. These forms, built on a giant scale using cutting-edge technologies, were conceived with the aim of representing the link with the past and tradition, but were also intended to express progress and the high degree of innovation that the countries have achieved.

At the end of the 1990s such forms were used to characterize the Petronas Towers, which adopted the geometric shapes and profile of a minaret; the Jin Mao Building, which recalls a pagoda; and the Tuntex Sky Tower, which alludes to the Chinese character *gao*, meaning "high" or "height." This approach continues to distinguish the most recent skyscrapers vying for the title of the world's highest building: Taipei 101, which is also inspired by a pagoda, and the Burj Dubai, which resembles a sort of ziggurat, rising by steps.

28 ◼ **The majestic Tuntex Sky Tower dominates the mainly low-rise urban fabric of Kaohsiung City with its gigantic form inspired by traditional forms.**

29 ◼ **The tower has a massive base and two separate 35-story sections, which merge in a central tower rising to a spire.**

30-31 ■ This drawing shows the building viewed from below. The central space that stabilizes the tower, reducing its mass and wind loads, can be seen in the foreground.

The Chinese-born architect C. Y. Lee appears to be a follower of this stylistic trend. His Tuntex Sky Tower dominates the Kaohsiung skyline with a silhouette created by combining and overlapping a series of elements belonging to the Chinese building tradition. It is formed of a solid base, which is raised higher than those of other similar buildings to allow tunnels to run beneath it at street level. The base supports two separate 35-story towers, topped by a central one that terminates in an antenna, 1140 ft (348 m) above the ground. A space is thus created between the two central towers, which reduces wind pressure and thus performs an important stabilizing function.

However, C. Y. Lee did not only feature traditional forms, but also incorporated the principles of *fengshui* in the design of the building. Due to the many different functions that it combines – offices, residential units, a shopping center, a hotel occupying the 37th to 70th floors, and an observation deck on the roof served by elevators capable of speeds of 33 ft (10 m) per second – the building is arranged around eight circulation cores that offer access to the various functions that it houses, allowing each of them to be independent of the others.

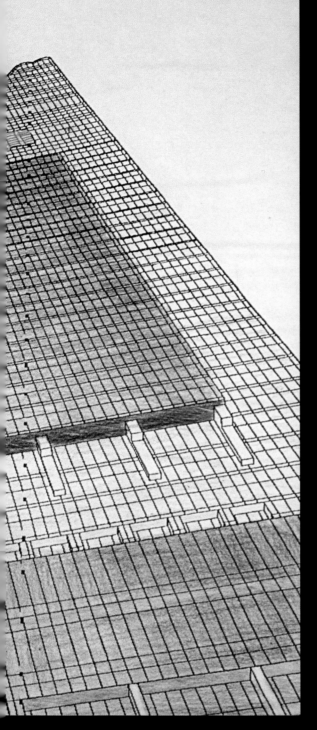

31 top right and bottom left ■ The east and north elevations show the building's massive profile, which was inspired by the Chinese character *gao*.

31 bottom right ■ The building's roof features Oriental style motifs that create parallels between the tower's image and those of the city's historic buildings.

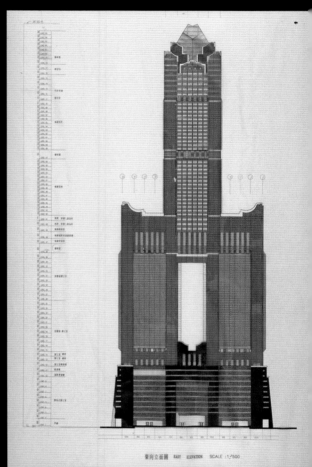

LOCATION	PROJECT	HEIGHT	FLOORS	YEAR
KAOHSIUNG - TAIWAN (THE REPUBLIC OF CHINA)	C.Y. LEE & PARTNERS	1140 FT 348 M	85	1997

MILLENNIUM TOWER

[VIENNA ■ AUSTRIA]

At 663 feet (including antenna), the Millennium Tower is the tallest building in Austria and one of the tallest in Europe – at least until the completion of the skyscrapers destined to redesign the City of London's skyline. Since its construction in 1999, the Millennium Tower has become the symbol of the population boom experienced by Vienna over the past 20 years, and the ensuing change in the city's urban planning policies. Indeed, during this period, the cautious conservatism that ensured architectural continuity with the old city, has been replaced with the desire to transform Vienna into a great modern metropolis, where the emphasis has shifted from the horizontal to the vertical dimension. Vienna's city government has responded to the population surge by

32 ■ **The Millennium Tower is topped by a smaller cylindrical volume superimposed on its summit and a regular parallelepiped cut at an angle that extends above it. It is crowned by two antennas, which bring the building's total height to 663 feet.**

33 ■ **The Millennium Tower stands on the bank of the Danube and its silhouette, formed by the intersection of two cylinders with a regular parallelepiped, has become the landmark of this part of the Austrian capital.**

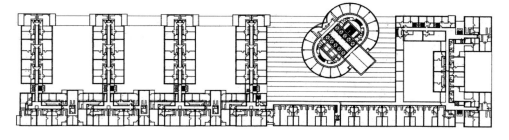

35 top ■ The tower is positioned asymmetrically at the point where the comb-shaped building loses its regularity to form a wider plaza. It is rotated so that part of its base juts out from the basement, allowing it to be accessed directly from the street.

raising the urban density ratio and building height limits in order to avoid reducing the capital's green areas. Consequently, since the 1990s, many skyscrapers have been built in the city, redesigning the areas surrounding the center. To the south Massimiliano Fuksas' Vienna Twin Towers forms an entrance gate to the city, while the main landmark to the north, along the right bank of the Danube and beyond, is the Millennium Tower. The building, designed by Peichl, Podrecca and Weber, is situated on the riverbank and has become the icon for the redesign and revitalization of the Brigittenau district, a strategic intermediate point between the city center and the areas across the Danube.

The tower is part of Vienna's Millennium City, a huge complex featuring buildings of different shapes and types. The tower has a rectangular 4-story basement running parallel to the river, which houses a parking area for 1500 cars, topped by a comb-shaped building comprising a double-level shopping center with 60 stores and 400 residential units on 4 floors. These elements are arranged to overlook the river and the large courtyards situated between the various buildings. The courtyards and the huge plaza on the basement roof create a network of public gardens and paved areas, where people can meet and relax. Other facilities and

34 ■ The basement containing the car park is topped by a comb-shaped building housing a shopping center and residential units.

35 bottom ■ The elevation shows the arrangement of the floors of the Millennium City: the lower ones are transparent, because they house the shopping centre, while the upper ones, marked by the bands of windows, are reserved for the residential units.

LOCATION	PROJECT	HEIGHT	FLOORS	YEAR
VIENNA (AUSTRIA)	GUSTAV PEICHL, BORIS PODRECCA AND RUDOLF F. WEBER	663 FT 202 M	51	1999

36-37 ■ The roof of the huge plaza on which the tower is set is completely glazed, allowing its striking dimensions can be perceived from inside.

services, including restaurants, banks and day-care centers, make the complex a city within the city, while a subway station, five urban railway lines and three bus routes offer easy access from the nearby districts and good links to the center. The tower, with 50 floors of offices, rises out of this well-structured multi-story basement. It is composed of three intersecting volumes: two cylinders housing the offices (featuring a mixture of individual and open-plan offices and collective areas); a rectangular prism containing the conference rooms; and a low cylinder on top of the prism, originally designed to house a hotel, but actually occupied by more offices.

The intersecting areas of the three elements house the circulation areas, escape stairs and nine elevators; while the services are enclosed in a load-bearing structure made from reinforced concrete that forms a central core. This is surrounded by a ring of steel and concrete pillars, which is linked to a second ring around the outer perimeter of the tower to form a structural frame. Its concentric layout allows it to withstand both vertical loads and horizontal pressure produced by wind or earthquakes. The framework is clad with aluminum and glass and characterized by a horizontal pattern. The specifications of the aluminum ensure the efficient heat insulation of the building, while the reflective glass has a built-in sun filter in order to reduce solar transmission. This metallic curtain wall and its sculptural form are the distinguishing characteristics of the tower, which dominates the skyline of the Danube Valley.

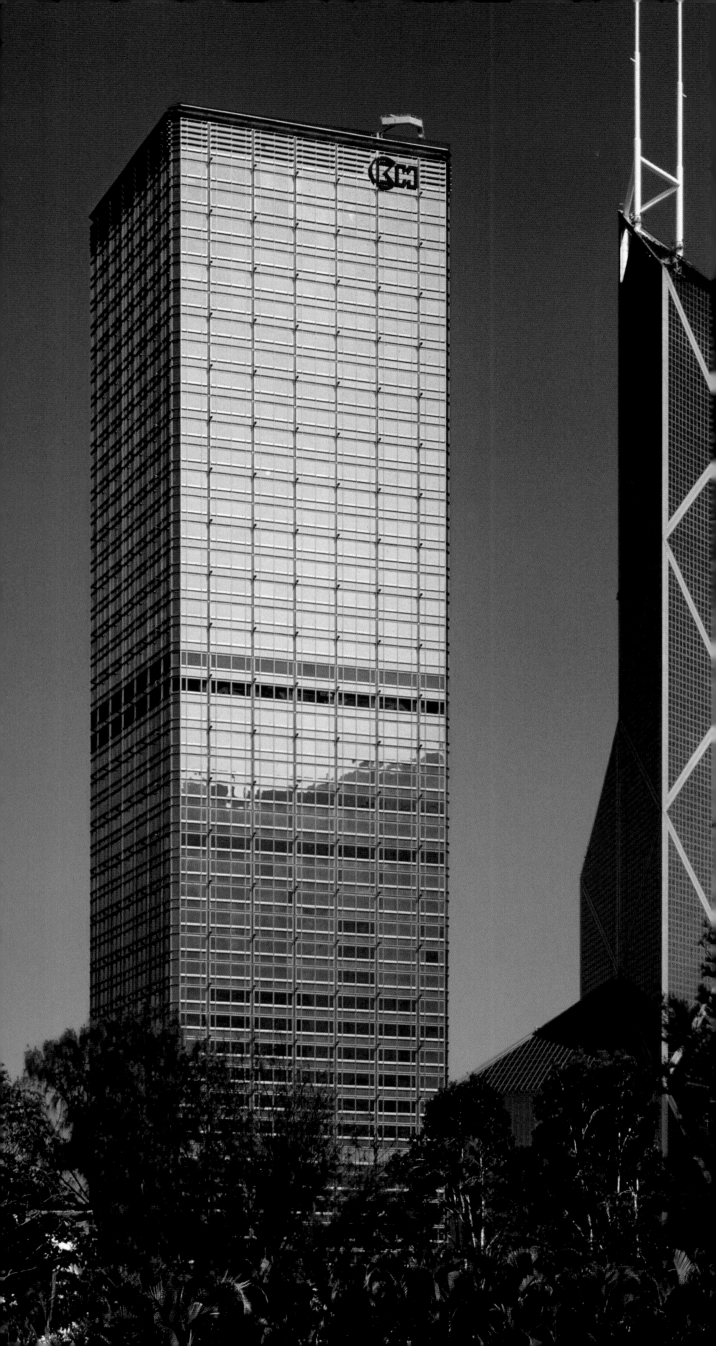

CHEUNG KONG CENTER

[HONG KONG ■ THE PEOPLE'S REPUBLIC OF CHINA]

American architect Cesar Pelli is world famous for his buildings that reinterpret historical forms using cutting-edge technologies. This strategy has proved to be particularly successful in the Asian metropolises that seek symbols associated with their traditions, but which are nonetheless capable of expressing their contemporary economic and financial prestige. Pelli's Hong Kong buildings propose two such archetypal figures: the monolithic prism for the Cheung Kong Center, and the stepped-back form for Two International Finance Centre.

The architect's choice to adopt these figures was based on several different factors: the exceptionally wide variety of forms in Hong Kong's urban landscape, local building regulations, the principles of *Fengshui*, and the innovative and iconic potential that these archetypal figures are capable of generating when constructed using state-of-the art materials and technologies. This is particularly evident in the Cheung

38 ■ The Cheung Kong Center boasts a simple abstract form, which is distinguished by an elegant steel grid encasing a reflective glass curtain wall.

39 ■ The complex silhouette of the Bank of China Tower, the floor pattern of the Cheung Kong Center and the design of the suspension trusses of the HSBC Main Building stand out on the night skyline.

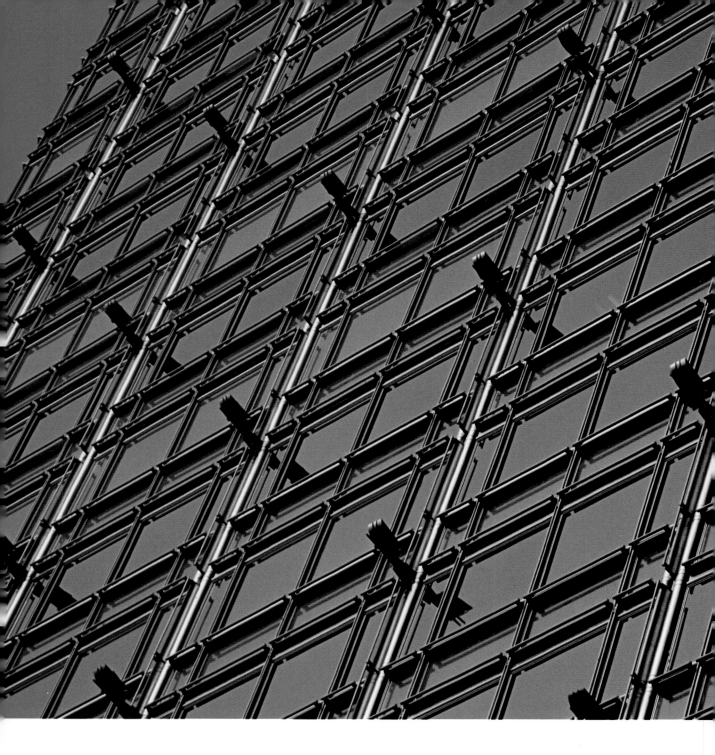

Kong Center, which is situated between Norman Foster's HSBC Main Building – one of the most novel high-tech skyscrapers, whose image is derived from the monumentality of its structural framework – and I. M. Pei's Bank of China Tower, in which a series of triangular frameworks follow a spiral pattern to create an original sculptural form. In order to stand out from these two buildings, Pelli's tower needed to have a simple, elegant form.

The regular prism replaced a former Hilton Hotel building, which was demolished to make space for the new headquarters of Cheung Kong Holdings, one of the city's leading property developers. The company's prestige is effectively conveyed by the striking image created by the building's distinctive cladding, which is its hallmark: a reflective glass curtain wall, which ensures the natural lighting of the interiors and allows its occupants to admire spectacular views of the bay, overlaid by a tubular stainless steel grid, which gleams on the Hong Kong skyline.

The grid is overlaid in turn by a network of optical fibers and spotlights, which completely change the building's appearance at night, when the spotlights illuminate the steel grid, underscoring the horizontal divisions and continuity of the façades, and the optical fibers can be programmed to color the surfaces of the tower or

LOCATION	PROJECT	HEIGHT	FLOORS	YEAR
HONG KONG (THE PEOPLE'S REPUBLIC OF CHINA)	DESIGN ARCHITECT: PELLI CLARKE PELLI ARCHITECTS - ASSOCIATE ARCHITECT: LEO A. DALY ARCHITECT OF RECORD: HSIN YIEH ARCHITECTS & ASSOCIATES LTD.	918 FT 280 M	62	1999

40-41 ■ This detail of the façade shows the tubular stainless steel grid that overlays the glass skin to define its image.

41 bottom ■ During the day, the tower's reflective glass skin allows its façade to change with the different colors of the sky and the elements that surround it.

form a 918-foot- high (280-m) liquid-crystal display. The trend to make the façades of buildings resemble large screens, stressing the media role attributed to architecture, is becoming increasingly widespread and has resulted in the emergence of the term "media buildings," i.e., structures whose main purpose is to broadcast information. In Pelli's building, the screens are not always visible, but when activated appear as a luminous lantern, like a lighthouse overlooking the harbor.

The complex exterior arrangement of the building contrasts with the simplicity of its square floor plan and layout of the interiors, which have been divided and oriented according to the principles of *Fengshui*, marking another way in which the Cheung Kong Center is tied to local tradition.

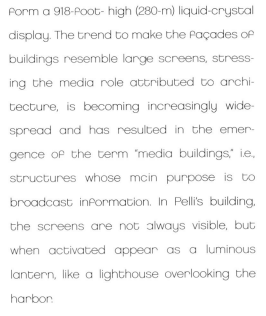

AURORA PLACE

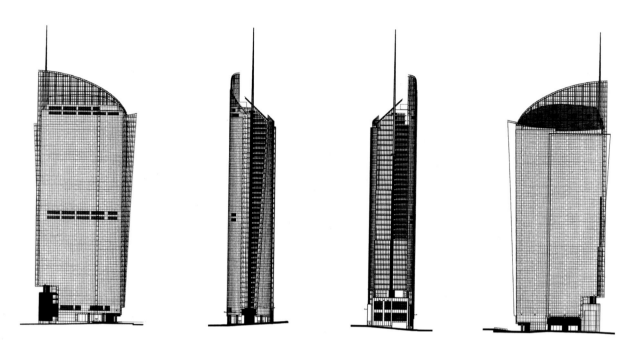

Renzo Piano's Aurora Place is located in central Sydney, on Macquarie Street, which marks the boundary of the city's financial district with an even wall of regularly shaped blocks. The street also runs alongside the Royal Botanic Gardens, and Jørn Utzon's Opera House beyond, reaching out toward the sea. Piano attempted to engage his building with this architectural icon by using plastic forms recalling the sails of the boats in the bay, which also provided the inspiration for Utzon's design. Indeed, the glass curtain walls that envelop Aurora Place are shaped like sails and extend above the actual building, emphasizing their lightness.

The complex was commissioned by the Lend Lease Development, the leading Australian property management and investment company, on occasion of the 2000 Olympic Games, and features two buildings: a 44-story office block and a 17-story residential block. The latter is situated on Macquarie Street and completes the compact wall of buildings overlooking the Gardens with its straight façade composed of a series of successive layers.

The first of these is a glazed membrane characterized by the slender design of its uprights and horizontal louvers. Behind this lies an empty layer formed by a continuous open gallery that occupies the entire height of the façade. When the membrane is closed this space extends the area of the individual apartments, becoming terraces overlooking the Gardens and the bay when it is open. The next layer is formed by the wall of the actual building, clad in terracotta, while the final one is the façade facing the tower, which takes the form of a curved glass surface, echoing those of the tower itself.

42 ■ This picture shows the various elevations of Renzo Piano's office tower.

43 ■ In the part that extends above the actual building, the top of the great glass curtain wall encasing Aurora Place assumes a superficial character that immediately evokes the sails of the boats in Sydney Harbour.

45 ■ Both towers of the complex are visible from Macquarie Street: the lower one housing the residential units overlooking the Botanic Gardens, and the taller one with the offices.

The forms and materials used for the stratified façade relate the building to its site as they feature several typical elements of the local architecture. Indeed, the open gallery is a reinterpretation of the theme of the Art Deco solarium and the colonial veranda, and its pattern is based on the spacing and division of the adjacent buildings. Similarly, the colors of the terracotta blend with the tones of the other structures lining Macquarie Street. The stratified façade allows the building to capture the sea breezes coming in from the Pacific and provides natural ventilation for the residential units behind it, thus saving energy.

The continuous effect that the residential block establishes with the wall of buildings overlooking the Royal Botanic Gardens is not repeated in the office tower. Indeed, its 656-foot (200-m) long façade on Phillip Street constitutes an autonomous entity that engages with a very different urban landscape, characterized by a series of tall towers that mark the edge of the financial district.

Piano's tower is developed prevalently along the vertical axis, which is enclosed by two curved walls that extend beyond it in order to make it appear bigger and thus able to compete with the much larger adjacent buildings, particularly Chifley Tower, designed by Kohn Pedersen Fox. Together with the latter, it seems to form a sort of gateway to the financial quarter.

The tower's curved glass surfaces differentiate it from the neighboring buildings and give it its singular character. These surfaces are independent of the central terracotta volume and the outside pillars that together form the tower structure.

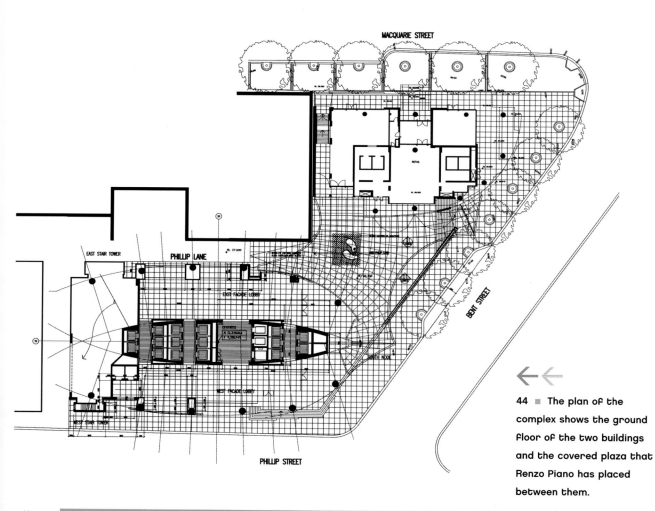

44 ■ The plan of the complex shows the ground floor of the two buildings and the covered plaza that Renzo Piano has placed between them.

LOCATION	PROJECT	HEIGHT	FLOORS	YEAR
SYDNEY (AUSTRALIA)	RENZO PIANO BUILDING WORKSHOP, ARCHITECTS	656 FT 200 M	44	2000

←←

46-47 ■ A transparent roof protects the public plaza lying between the two towers.

As they have no visible frame, from a distance they appear as uniform surfaces, although their opacity actually varies according to the diameters of the small white ceramic circles positioned between the panels of the façades and the distances between them. The same panel may thus have completely different uses, such as a transparent window allowing spectacular views, an opaque parapet to cover the service areas or hide the pattern of the floors, or an opaque screen to reduce solar transmission. The infinite possibilities for gradation of opacity and transparency allow the façade enormous potential for constant change. However, this is not fully exploited, for the opaque and transparent panels are not positioned to create an overall effect, but following the functional reasons described above. Consequently, the arrangement of the façade corresponds to the division of the areas behind it. The initial image of the sail used by Piano to echo the design of the Opera House is thus transformed into a more traditional curtain wall marked by horizontal bands of windows, like that of many surrounding buildings. Nonetheless, the form of the wall distinguishes the tower from the other structures, for the two curved glass surfaces do not form a single volume and are repeatedly deformed to create a complex ensemble. The north façade completely covers the terracotta core, while the south one allows it to emerge and is twisted and set back at the base to create a public plaza. This area, covered with a transparent glass roof supported by a lightweight mesh structure, connects the two towers and allows access to the complex.

Although this public space is enclosed within a transparent perimeter, which allows visual continuity between the interior and exterior of the building, it is actually an extension of the street, allowing the site to be crossed and offering a seamless pedestrian link to Circular Quay, which is emphasized by the use of the parterre.

↑
↑

47 top ■ The columns of the tower are clad in terracotta, like the building behind them.

47 bottom ■ The curved wall that forms the main façade is broken in front of the entrances to Aurora Place in order to extend the public area at the base of the building.

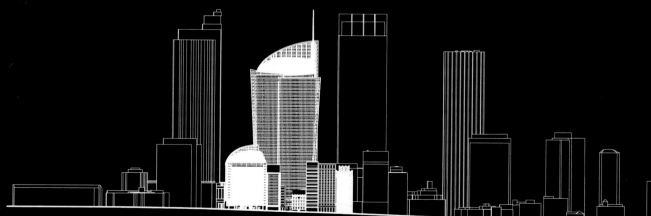

48-49 bottom ■ The section along Macquarie Street shows how the different dimensions of the two towers designed by Piano – the taller office block and the lower residential one overlooking the Botanic Gardens – are dependent on the relationship of the former with the skyscrapers of the financial district, while both engage with Utzon's Opera House through their sail-shaped façade.

48-49 top ■ The interiors are
defined by the same materials
used for the exterior, making them
warm and welcoming: terracotta
and glass, combined with wood
for the floors and furnishings.

49 ■ A detail of the glass skin
that encloses the galleries of the
residential tower overlooking the
Botanic Gardens.

VIENNA TWIN TOWERS

[VIENNA ■ AUSTRIA]

In 2001 Vienna acquired a new landmark: the Twin Towers, designed by Italian architect Massimiliano Fuksas. The building appears as a gateway to the capital to those approaching it from the south on the Triester Straße, the road connecting Vienna to the Italian city of Trieste, once the main seaport of the Austro-Hungarian Empire.

Vienna's skyline has changed greatly over the past 20 years, following the building boom that accompanied the opening of the Eastern European markets, Austria's entry to the European Union and the policies of the city government, which decided to increase building density by expanding the city upward rather than encroaching on its green areas. It was against this backdrop that a competition was launched for the redevelopment of the old Weinerberger industrial district on the southern outskirts of the city; an area characterized by the world's most famous brick factory and the Philips House, a reinforced concrete structure built by architect Karl Schwanzer in the 1960s.

The competition was won by Fuksas, who was entrusted with the task of drawing up the new plan for the area, featuring a new residential district and a business center, for which he also designed the architecture. This took the form of twin towers set on a trapezoidal base.

The Italian architect employed the form of the double tower, which is one of the most frequently recurring forms in high-rise construction. This iconic form was used for the World Trade Center in Manhattan, whose towers have become even more

50 right ■ The sketch shows the two towers positioned at an angle of 59 degrees to each other.

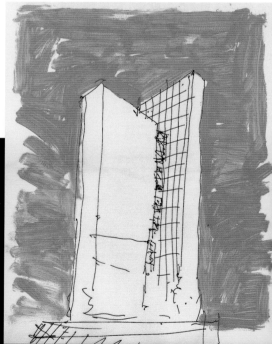

50 left ■ As can also be seen in the previous drawing, the towers are connected by bridges, creating the effect of a gateway to the city.

51 ■ The towers appear light and almost dematerialized, due to their unbroken glass façade supported by a frame so slender as to be almost imperceptible.

present in the public imagination following the dramatic events of 9/11 and their definitive collapse, and also for the Petronas Towers in Kuala Lumpur, which intentionally echoed their New York counterparts (thus underscoring the superiority of the Malaysian towers in terms of both height and image, reflecting the shift of global economic and commercial power from West to East). Finally, a pair of inclined towers – albeit on a smaller scale – mark the entrance to Madrid.

Doubling a tower by building a twin and creating a connection between the two structures creates the image of an urban gateway or monumental entrance, reworking the city gate as a sort of contemporary triumphal arch. This was the effect intended by Fuksas, who chose the image to mark the end of the Triester Straße. The two towers are not exactly identical: the first has 37 stories and is 453 ft (138 m) tall, while the second has 34 stories and is 417 ft (127 m) tall. However, both are regular prisms and completely transparent. After careful calculations, the towers were positioned at an angle of 59 degrees to each other in order to offer ever-changing views from various points of the city.

The simple form and all-glass façades of the building inevitably invite parallels with Mies van der Rohe's glass skyscrapers of the 1920s and his later American works, particularly the Lake Shore Drive Apartments in Chicago. The latter are twin towers with a rectangular plan, placed at an angle of 90 degrees to each other. The main difference between the two landmarks lies in the technology and design of their skin: Mies' towers are characterized by the pattern formed by the upright of their frames,

52 ■ **The towers are completely transparent regular prisms, positioned at an angle of 59 degrees to each other in order to offer ever-changing views from various points of the city. They are different heights, with the tallest one rising 36 ft (11 m) above its twin.**

53 ■ **This cross section of the tallest tower also shows the base housing the large double-height atrium, and various facilities: a cinema, stores and plant rooms.**

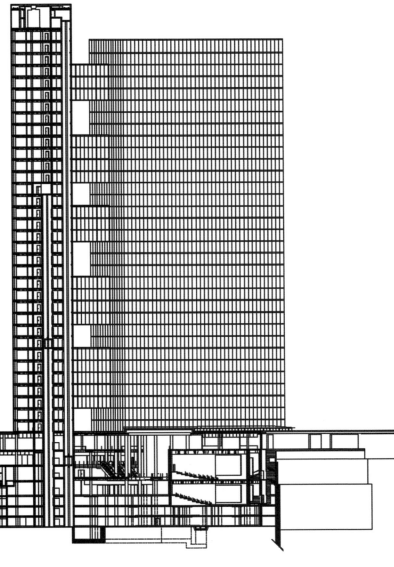

LOCATION	PROJECT	HEIGHT	FLOORS	YEAR
VIENNA (AUSTRIA)	MASSIMILIANO FUKSAS	453 FT (138 M) 417 FT (127 M)	37 34	2001

which gives them a heavy, monolithic appearance, while Fuksas' ones seem light and almost dematerialized, due to their unbroken glass façade whose frame is so slender as to be almost imperceptible. This dematerialized image – reminiscent of the impression created by Jean Nouvel in his works in which transparency mingles with reflective, stratified and disintegrated effects – characterizes the Vienna Twin Towers and their base. Transparent walls enclose the latter, so that the inner space is extremely permeable from the outside and at the same time open and expanded, for most of it is double height. It is covered by a solid concrete surface that extends over the entire plot, whose trapezoidal shape it echoes, and features a hole that allows visitors to catch glimpses and views of the towers, which are entered through the base itself. In addition to the building's circulation areas, the base also houses various facilities: a cinema, stores and service rooms, thus satisfying all the necessary requirements for an efficient office block, but with an unusual layout and spaciousness for a business building, where quantitative considerations often take priority over spatial ones.

 54-55 ■ **The bridges connecting the two towers are entirely glazed, in keeping with the image of the two towers.**

55 top ■ The roof of the base features a large aperture covered with a glass skylight, making the area below extremely well lit and allowing views of the towers from inside.

55 bottom left ■ The complex is accessed via a public plaza protected by the roof of the base, which extends beyond the actual building.

55 bottom right ■ The large atrium is characterized by many double-height areas, crossed by escalators connecting the various levels.

56-57 ■ The drawing shows the large aperture in the roof of the base, through which visitors can enjoy spectacular views of the towers.

57 top ■ This sketch shows the tower's crown.

57 bottom ■ The plan
of one of the stories shows
its simple layout featuring
a central core and a system
of columns arranged around
the perimeter.

→→

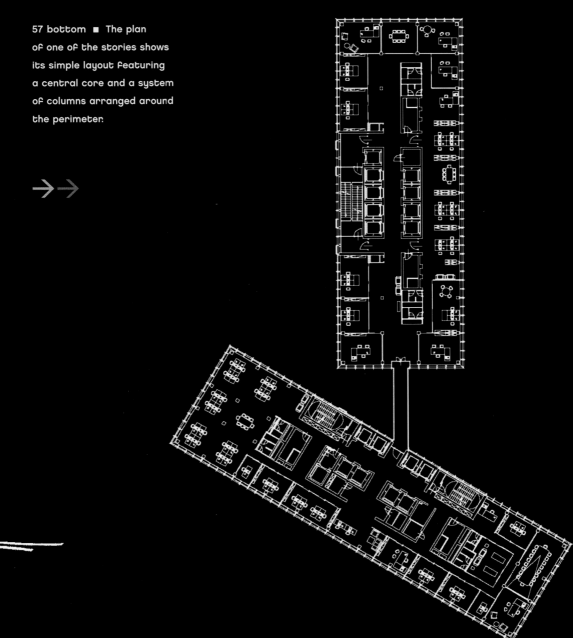

TRUMP WORLD TOWER

[NEW YORK ■ USA]

The Trump World Tower rises on the Manhattan skyline as a pure, slender, abstract geometric form. Designed by Costas Kondylis and Partners, at the time of construction the tower was the tallest all-residential building in the world, rising 861 ft (262 m). It stands on a small rectangular plot on First Avenue, between 47th and 48th Streets, and has a simple shape without any eccentric crowns, cusps, steps or any of the other distinguishing exterior features that have contributed to creating a varied cityscape bristling with bizarre figures, but also many International Style blocks. The architect drew on the most famous of these – the Seagram Building and the United Nations Headquarters – reinterpreting their image in a contemporary style and thus giving precedence to the desire for height over the importance of maintaining the balanced proportions of this building type. The result is that the Trump World Tower appears out of place in its setting – characterized by many International Style monoliths – due to its disproportionate shape.

The immense height of the building was made possible by the acquisition of air rights of the adjacent properties, which were added to those of the plot. This stratagem was subsequently made impossible by new building regulations; consequently the current skyline and the status of the Trump World Tower as the city's highest all-residential building will remain unaltered. In order to achieve this height the architect had to find structural solutions capable of withstanding wind and seismic loads. The structure is composed of two large load-bearing walls. The elevator shafts are built against the southern one and 27 columns are arranged around the perimeter of the tower. The size and number of these massive columns varies from the base to the summit of the building, and although they occupy much of the plan they are invisible from the outside.

58 ■ The triangular profile of the Citigroup Center, the simple slender form of the Trump World Tower and the lower, squatter silhouette of the United Nations Headquarters rise on the Manhattan skyline.

59 ■ The pure, abstract form of the tower and its simple crown contrast with the greatest icons of the Manhattan landscape: the antenna of the Empire State Building and the spire of the Chrysler Building.

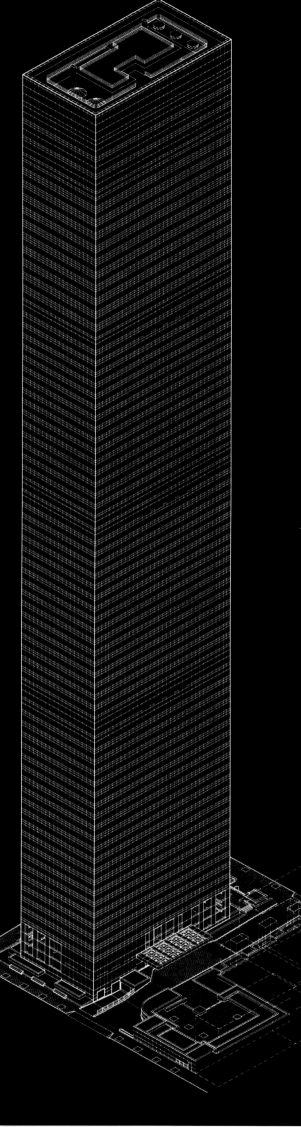

60 ■ This axonometric projection of the building shows the structure of its base.

60-61 ■ This view from the ground emphasizes the evenness of the tower's skin, achieved by the lack of visible joints and the effects produced by the use of bronze-colored reflective glass.

LOCATION	PROJECT	HEIGHT	FLOORS	YEAR
NEW YORK (USA)	COSTAS KONDYLIS & PARTNERS	861 FT 262 M	72	2001

At the time of construction the size of the new tower aroused much opposition, mainly due to the concern that it would dwarf the nearby United Nations Headquarters, considered a symbolic building. However, others, weary of eccentric forms, Art Deco-style buildings, excessive decoration and the Disneyland-like constructions that had recently invaded the area around Times Square, applauded the choice of such a simple austere style.

Despite its resemblance to International Style skyscrapers, the elegant appearance of the Trump World Tower is not only due to its height and slender proportions, but also to its glass curtain wall. Unlike its predecessors, whose exterior appearance was conditioned by the thickness of their walls, the façade of the Trump World Tower appears as an unbroken surface, giving the building a monolithic look and creating the impression of a "single sheet of glass" rising out of the ground, as intended by Kondylis. Its appearance is rendered even more uniform and abstract by the use of bronze-colored reflective glass – the stylistic hallmark of Donald Trump's various buildings, which ensures that the interiors are well lit and enjoy breathtaking views.

In addition to residential units of various sizes, the tower is also home to a series of open and green areas, basements, a four-star restaurant on the ground floor, and a fitness center with 82-foot swimming pools destined for its famous residents. Indeed, Bill Gates, Sophia Loren and Harrison Ford were among the first to purchase an apartment in the building. The interiors of the tower were thus designed to satisfy an exclusive clientele and contrast with the elegant simplicity of its exterior. Their lavish materials and sumptuous décor evoke those of the early skyscrapers, which emphasized their separateness from the world of the street by flaunting and symbolizing the wealth and power of their owners with rich decorations, statues and polychrome marble.

PLAZA 66

The widespread diffusion of skyscrapers has profoundly altered the metropolitan skylines of both the Western and Eastern worlds with a profusion of bizarre forms, including erotic gherkins, pyramids and technological pagodas. The Plaza 66 complex by Kohn Pedersen Fox Associates, built in Shanghai in 2001, combines several of these to form a multipurpose structure that is a collage of distinct geometric volumes. This arrangement is not purely formal or functional, despite the fact that each volume has a different purpose, for it was intended to reinterpret the complexity of the metropolis, the many different scales within it and the dynamism of the street along which the complex is situated: Nanjing Road West, one of the oldest and busiest shopping streets in central Shanghai. The assembly of shapes is dominated by curves, both concave and convex, which were chosen to express the vitality of the city, likened to a vortex.

The building features a base housing public areas, a shopping center, cultural and leisure facilities and an underground car park. It is arranged around a curved

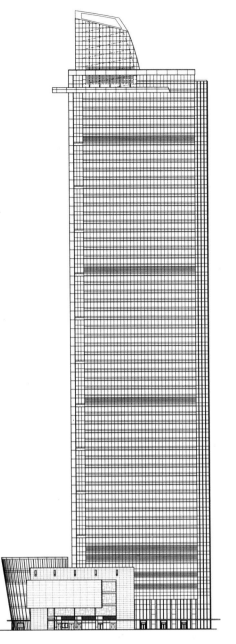

63 top ■ The eastern elevation shows the volume through which the building is accessed on the left and the tallest tower on the right.

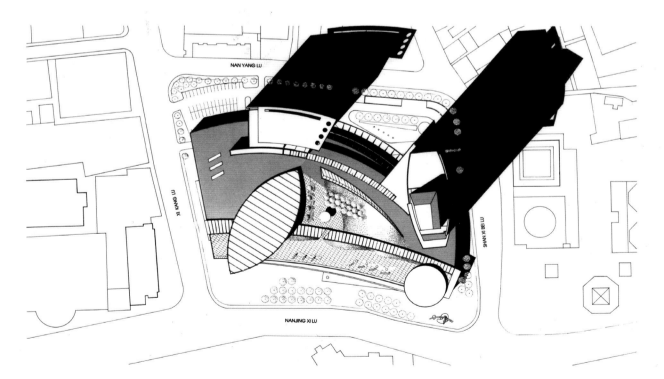

62 ■ The tower is crowned by a glass volume that creates its distinctive silhouette.

63 bottom ■ The volumetric plan of the complex shows the composite structure of Plaza 66: the two towers at the top, the two entrance halls at the bottom – the first with an almond-shaped plan and the second with a circular plan – connected by a glass-roofed arcade.

64 ■ The inside of the lantern on the top of the tallest tower.

64-65 ■ The interiors of the shopping centre are arranged on five floors connected by escalators and lit from above by large skylights.

arcade that terminates in the two entrance areas, marked by glazed volumes that jut out from the podium, becoming luminous lanterns at night. One is almond shaped, while the other has the form of an upturned cone. These volumes not only differ in shape, but also in size and materials, allowing each to engage with the various elements of the contemporary metropolis. The base has five stories and is clad with stone, with the exception of the entrances halls and arcade, which are made of glass. The use of this material and the height of the base contrast with the fabric of the traditional Chinese city, while the towers maintain a dialogue with the vertical urban landscape that started to be superimposed on the original one during the 1990s, occupying even the most central areas of Shanghai.

The two towers follow the same compositional approach as the rest of the complex, for they are not simple volumes, but three-dimensional aggregations of parts.

LOCATION	PROJECT	HEIGHT	FLOORS	YEAR
SHANGHAI (THE PEOPLE'S REPUBLIC OF CHINA)	KOHN PEDERSEN FOX ASSOCIATES	945 FT 288 M	66	2001

65 bottom ■ This detail of the base viewed from the street clearly shows the different volumes and the materials that distinguish them: glass for the entrances and stone for the rest.

The tallest one stands against the base and forms its east façade, through which the tower is accessed. Its cross-section has the form of an almond without the corners and the tower is enclosed in a glass skin. The east façade is marked by a horizontal pattern, while the west façade has a vertical design. The tower culminates in a lantern that is illuminated at night and can be seen from afar, making the building appear slimmer and slenderer. Its structural elements take the form of a reinforced concrete central core that houses the circulation and service areas and a ring of large circular columns placed around the perimeter.

A second tower, with 45 floors, was built in 2006. This volume is separate from the base and has a sloping top, surmounted by a roof at the same angle. The main structure, covered with a glass curtain wall, contains two smaller volumes: a vertical one, rotated and positioned asymmetrically, and a horizontal one at the base of the former, from which a curved bridge connects it to the taller tower.

66-67 ■ The many glazed elements of the base housing the public facilities – including the entrance hall in the shape of an upturned cone – allow the interior of the building to engage with the exterior.

 ←←

67 bottom ■ At night, Plaza 66 can be distinguished on the Shanghai skyline by the lantern on its roof, which characterizes its slender soaring silhouette.

←←

TOUR EDF

[PARIS ■ FRANCE]

The Tour EDF (the headquarters of France's main electricity company) by Henry N. Cobb is situated in La Défense, a former industrial area on the outskirts of Paris that commenced its transformation into a major business and financial district during the 1960s. It reached its height in the 1980s, under François Mitterrand's government, when the building regulations were changed to allow the construction of tall towers with the purpose of creating a new administrative center in Paris, structured according to the same rules adopted by Baron Haussmann during the 19th century. Indeed, it is laid out along a major corridor, in this case the extension of the monumental *Axe Historique* connecting the Louvre and the Arc de Triomphe via the Champs-Élysées. Johann Otto von Spreckelsen's Grande Arche, built in 1989, is the symbol of this operation and marks the end of the axis. The Danish architect's design was chosen because it expressed the desire for monumentality and continuity with the past, offering a modern reinterpretation of the Napoleonic triumphal arch in the form of a 361-ft (110-m) cube with its center removed to form a giant gateway. The Tour EDF stands in a prime position on the axis, for it is the first tall building visible from the Grande Arche. Furthermore, the view of the latter from the base of the tower is even more striking for this stretch of the corridor is an elevated pedestrian area, known as La Dalle.

68 ■ The Tour EDF is situated in a strategic position along Paris' monumental *Axe historique* that connects the Grande Arche in La Défense with the Louvre, via the Arc de Triomphe.

69 ■ The volume of the acute-angled tower is deformed, creating a convex façade in the point where it intersects the *Axe historique* with which La Défense is aligned.

70 ■ The convex façade continues up to the 26th floor, at the same height as the top of the void in the cube of the Grande Arche, where the acute angle that also distinguishes its rear elevation reappears.

LOCATION	PROJECT	HEIGHT	FLOORS	YEAR
PARIS (FRANCE)	HENRY N. COBB	486 FT 148 M	41	2002

The Tour EDF stands out from the urban landscape of La Défense, characterized by numerous rectangular blocks, due to its sculptural volume, whose form, proportions and position are the result of its close engagement with its setting and the Grande Arche in particular. The architect chose a sculptural figure, created by the extrusion of an elliptical form, and positioned it in such a way that its longitudinal axis is parallel to the Grande Arche, which instead of standing perpendicular to the corridor connecting it to the Arc de Triomphe and central Paris, is turned at an angle of 6.33 degrees, so that it is viewed slightly skewed.

The short side of the Tour EDF, ending in an acute angle, overlooks the *Axe Historique* and has a conical shape carved into it up to level 26, at the same height as the top of the void in the cube of the Grande Arche. This missing part, which seems to have been cut out of the building at its intersection with La Dalle, makes the façade concave and gives it a more sculptural appearance, as well as creating a public entrance area to the tower.

The space is covered with a thin steel canopy measuring 79 ft (24 m) in diameter, creating a pleasant meeting place that also offers shelter from the rain and an extraordinary view of the plaza and the Grande Arche.

The structural elements of the building consist of a reinforced concrete core with the same elliptical form, which houses the tower's circulation and service areas, and a series of reinforced concrete columns around the perimeter.

The tower's imposing appearance is the result of the combined effect of its sculptural form and its distinctive façade, formed by a curtain wall with alternating bands of gleaming bronze-colored stainless steel and reflective glass panels.

The same elements were reused by Pei Cobb Freed & Partners in the recent Hyatt Center in Chicago, but without the most distinctive feature of the Parisian tower: the conical shape carved into the main façade, which creates a close bond between the building and its setting.

71 top ■ The sculptural form of the Tour EDF is created by the extrusion of an elliptical shape and distinguishes it from the other buildings of La Défense.

71 bottom ■ The entrance to the tower is covered with a circular steel canopy that protects the public space in front of it.

DONGBU FINANCIAL CENTER

[SEOUL ∎ SOUTH KOREA]

Despite the constantly growing number of skyscrapers designed by Kohn Pedersen Fox Associates all over the world, the international architectural design firm does not employ a predetermined formula for its high-rise buildings, but defines the structural form of each project according to the unique characteristics of its location, the requests of the client and also functional requirements.

The compositional principle adopted for the Dongbu Financial Center in Seoul, which determines its image, structure and arrangement, is a method traditionally used in a local handicraft, *shik-tak-bo*, which consists of sewing together a variety of fabrics in a random fashion, thus forming a series of layers and successive levels. The adoption of this process, derived from a field far removed from architecture, allowed the architects to associate the building with the local traditions and culture, but also to create an innovative form that stands out from the others surrounding it.

The Dongbu Financial Center is the headquarters of a leading Korean insurance company and is situated in the Kangnam-ku district on Seoul's Teheran Road, one of the city's main business streets, lined with a series of office blocks with simple, regular geometric shapes. The architects wished to interrupt the repetitiveness and rigidity of the existing architecture by inserting a dynamic form in its midst, thus expressing the vitality and economic growth of the city and the entire country. The continuity of the street front was also broken – despite the small dimensions of the area – by setting the building back to create a

← →

72 ∎ **The distinctive form of the Dongbu Financial Center is achieved by the use of successive layers, each inclined at a different angle, which form various overlapping volumes.**

73 ∎ **The longitudinal section shows the regularity of the floors of the tower, with the exception of the base, where the large atrium connects the street level to the basement floors housing a shopping mall and a subway station via wide escalators.**

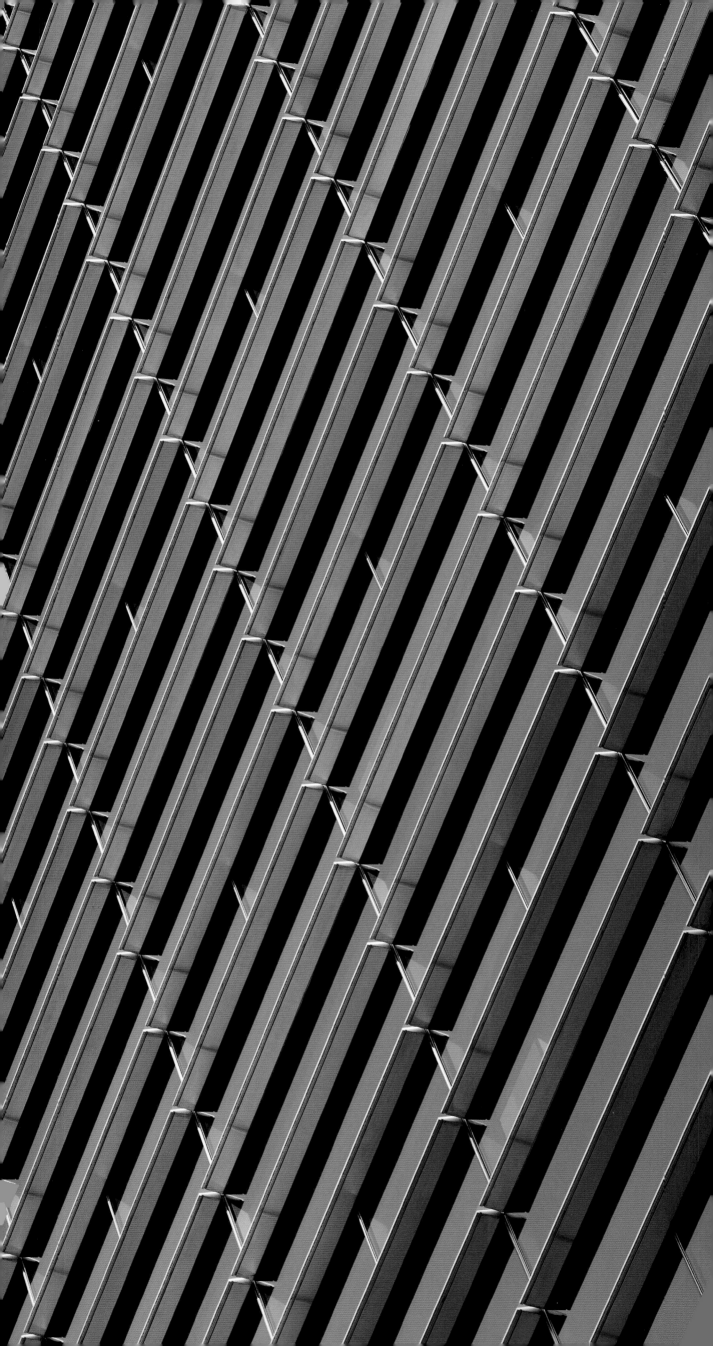

74-75 ■ The blue reflective glass panels of the tower's façade are overlaid with a stainless steel brise-soleil system that forms a closely spaced horizontal pattern.

75 ■ The building's original and dynamic form interrupts the street front – characterized by regular rectangular blocks – of Teheran Road, one of Seoul's main business streets.

LOCATION	PROJECT	HEIGHT	FLOORS	YEAR
SEOUL (SOUTH KOREA)	KOHN PEDERSEN FOX ASSOCIATES	495 FT 151 M	35	2012

public plaza across which it is approached and entered. This square is furnished with seats, trees, lamps and a wall – a frame holding glass fragments, also inspired by *shik-tak-bo* – which delineates the base of the tower, constituting a buffer area between the activities of the street and those of the large atrium housed inside. The wall through which the light filters gives this area a particularly warm and welcoming atmosphere, which is reinforced by the lavish use of wood and limestone that recalls the luxurious foyers of the early American skyscrapers. Escalators connect this huge, stratified hollow space to a shopping center and a subway station located below street level.

The structure and layout of the entire building are achieved by the use of successive layers, as in *shik-tak-bo*, determining the arrangement of its volumes, its floor plan, its section and its main façade. Unlike Plaza 66 in Shanghai, in which KPF assembled a collage of pure geometric (and mainly curved) solids set in a base, the various parts of the Dongbu Financial Center do not remain independent, but are recomposed to form a complex volume, or rather a single volume that is broken down into parts. These constituent elements are successive surfaces, rather than volumes, which are stratified, inclined and extended beyond the limits of the building to emphasize their flat nature, revealing a clear sense of direction and hierarchy between the façades. The sense of direction is determined by the rectangular shape of the plot and the

76-77 ■ The base of the tower is set back from the other buildings forming the street front of Teheran Road. This allowed the architects to create a public square, furnished with seats, trees, lamps and a wall that delineates the base of the tower and creates a buffer area between the street and the large atrium.

77 top ■ The entrance to the tower is situated on its short side and takes the form of a bridge over a pool at the building's base.

77 bottom ■ The design of the wall evokes a local craft technique known as *shik-tak-bo*, which consists of sewing together a variety of fabrics in a random fashion.

architects' choice to use a part of it to create the plaza in front of the building, which further reinforces the extension of the façade overlooking the street and that opposite it in relation to the others.

The same compositional principle is employed to articulate the main façade through using a series of surfaces inclined at different angles, making it plastic and dynamic, and the reflective blue glass and stainless steel cladding that forms a closely spaced horizontal pattern. The same curtain wall also characterizes the opposite side of the tower, although this time with a single vertical surface. The two short sides, on the north and south of the building, have smooth transparent glass façades, behind which the pattern of the floors can be seen. The floor plan is arranged according to the same succession of parallel parts and volumes: the structural core and the circulation areas are positioned on the west side, instead of in the center, in order to allow greater space on the façade overlooking the street and the park.

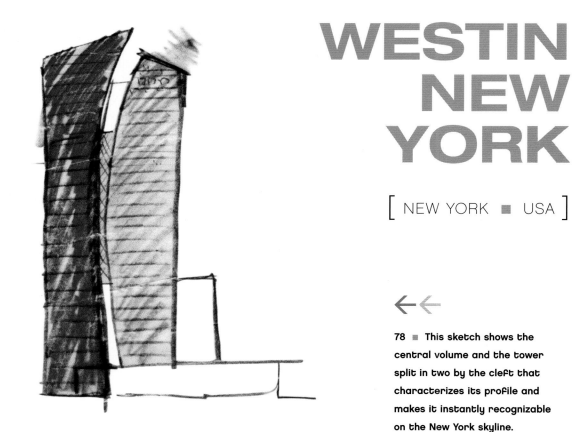

WESTIN NEW YORK

[NEW YORK ■ USA]

←←

Arquitectonica's first building in New York City is the Westin New York, situated in Times Square, between 42nd and 43rd Streets and 7th and 8th Avenues. In 1994 the Miami-based architectural firm won the competition (whose entrants also included Michael Graves and Zaha Hadid) for the transformation of the entire Times Square area.

The Westin New York was completed in 2002 and immediately provoked much controversy, receiving fierce criticism from those weary of garish and overly flamboyant architectural language and acclaim from those considering it to embody the spirit of Times Square. Indeed, large luminous signs and billboards have always characterized the city's theater district, making it an area in which architecture and graphic design have long merged to form a single expressive medium. It is in this type of city – strongly distinguished by billboards, lights, advertising, images and electronic script, and constituted by buildings whose façades are enormous sets – that Arquitectonica finds the most fertile ground for inspiration. As always, the Latin American origins of Bernardo Fort-Brescia, who founded the firm's together with his wife Laurinda Spear, are clearly visible in this project, along with the influence of Mexican architect Luis Barragán and his use of color and combination of geometric forms.

The Times Square building is profoundly different from the group of International Style towers that stand around it, but also from the Condé Nast Building, which despite sharing the feature of a base housing displays and billboards, is defined by two regular rectangular blocks. It is also distinguished from Renzo Piano's New York Times Building, a slender form with elegant glass and ceramic façades. The Westin, on the other hand, is arranged like a collage of different volumes with diverse shapes, materials and functions.

79 ■ The tower is clad with panels of reflective glass, which are colored in shades of blue and create a vertical pattern in the upper part and form a horizontal design in tones of bronze in the lower part.

→→

The two lowest volumes allow the building to engage with the street, while the tower relates it to the sky and an intermediate element connects the various forms. The entire street-level structure is characterized by displays, images and billboards and has two separate volumes: that on the corner between 43rd Street and 8th Avenue is a single structure housing the hotel bar, while that on 42nd Street is a shopping mall known as the E-Walk, which also contains theaters and restaurants, and has a broken façade composed of a series of small buildings.

The E-Walk is a new kind of shopping center, arranged along an inner walkway entirely overlooking the street, where the entrances to the stores are located. It is arranged on several levels, including basements, with the theaters situated on the upper levels, accessible by large elevators.

The intermediate part of the building between the base and the tower is an autonomous volume housing 150 hotel rooms, defined on each side by a zigzagging surface that appears to have been folded. The façades are characterized by a series of identically sized windows arranged like a checkerboard and by the irregular design of the cladding, with panels in various earth tones.

The tower is split in two by a curving beam of light that cuts through the entire height of the building and continues into the sky. The two parts have different heights, shapes and materials, continuing the collage theme that distinguishes the entire building.

The taller part curves over the lower one, as though embracing it. Both are clad with panels of reflective glass: varying shades of blue (from navy to azure and turquoise) arranged to form a vertical pattern for the taller one, and shades of bronze forming a horizontal pattern for the lower one. The cleft dividing the tower in two, the different heights of the parts, and the form of the roof create a very distinctive silhouette on the bristling Manhattan skyline.

80-81 ■ **The Westin perfectly expresses the spirit of Times Square and harmonizes with its setting with its wealth of shapes, colors and materials.** → →

LOCATION	PROJECT	HEIGHT	FLOORS	YEAR
NEW YORK (USA)	ARQUITECTONICA	526 FT 160 M	45	2002

82-83 and 83 ■ Like the building's exterior, its interior are also characterized by colorec materials, reflecti surfaces and alternating effects of light and shade.

DEUTSCHE POST TOWER

[BONN ■ GERMANY]

Architects Murphy/Jahn proposed a dynamic tower characterized by a transparent glass skin for the new Deutsche Post headquarters in Bonn, which contrasts with the post-modern forms and traditional materials of their previous projects, including the MesseTurm in Frankfurt (1990). This change in architectural language was already evident in the Sony Center in Berlin, which also boasts a transparent façade, but in the case of the Bonn building glass is used to form a double skin. This creates reflections and dematerialized effects, giving the Deutsche Post Tower an extremely innovative image, due to its ability to change continuously according to the different angle of the natural light and the various hues that it assumes when the colored lights are switched on between the two transparent surfaces. The innovative, intriguing new Deutsche Post headquarters have thus redesigned the landscape of the border area between the outskirts of Bonn and the huge park that lies along the banks of the Rhine.

The tower is the expression of an intermediate state between the natural and the manmade, for it creates a series of terraces and paths sloping towards the Rhine, ending in a covered plaza at the base of the tower, in which other natural elements are featured.

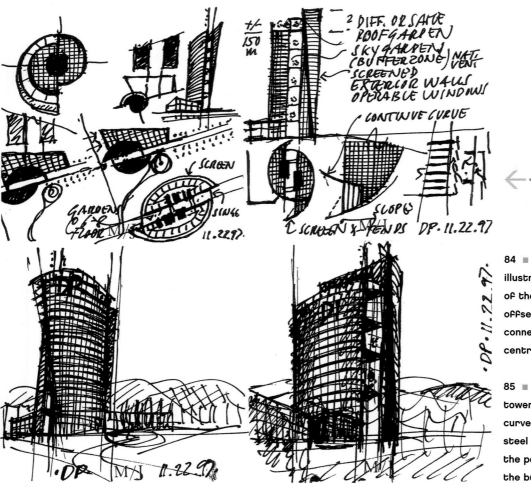

84 ■ The design sketches illustrate the composition of the tower, formed by two offset semicircular volumes connected by a large central void.

85 ■ The form of the tower is defined by two curved surfaces with a steel frame that supports the panels of glass encasing the building.

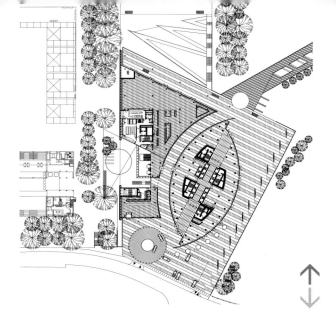

86 top ■ The plan of the low structure and the tower reveals that the latter is composed of two semicircular volumes. The circulation shafts are positioned along the huge space between them.

86 bottom ■ The entrance to the tower is protected by a metal canopy.

86-87 ■ The introduction of natural elements to the covered plaza at the base of the tower allows the natural dimension (which continues outside in a series of terraces and paths sloping towards the Rhine) to penetrate the interior of the building.

The presence of natural features in the interiors and devices that make the building an example of sustainable architecture, combined with the Post Tower's structure and image, allow it to be defined as a perfect synergy of architecture, technology and art.

The building is composed of two slightly offset semicircular volumes, positioned either side of a central void measuring about 23 ft (7 m) across. This space is crossed by a series of bridges connecting the two parts, along which the circulation shafts are positioned. The void, which extends through the entire height of the tower, together with skygardens on every ninth floor, allows the formation of air currents that provide natural ventilation, thus reducing the building's energy consumption and avoiding the need for cumbersome, unattractive ducts.

The large central area also allows the occupants to meet, talk or simply enjoy the views.

LOCATION	PROJECT	HEIGHT	FLOORS	YEAR
BONN (GERMANY)	ARCHITECT OF RECORD: MURPHY/JAHN SITE ARCHITECT: HEINLE, WISCHER UND PARTNER	533 FT 163 M	42	2002

87 bottom ■ The lobby opens up at the foot of the large space that connects the two parts of the tower.

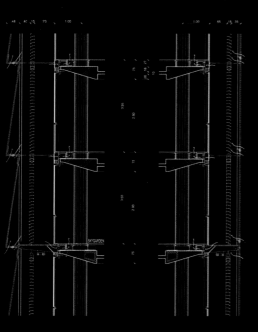

88 top left ■ The façade, seen here in a sectional view, is composed of two layers of glass and an outer layer of brises-soleils.

88 bottom left ■ The huge void that connects the two parts of the tower can be seen in the center of the cross section.

88 top right ■ The workspaces are flooded with natural light and offer spectacular views towards the river.

88 bottom right ■ The large central space is crossed by a series of bridges connecting the two parts, along which the circulation shafts are positioned.

89 ■ A detailed picture of the brise-soleil system of the façade and the 12-inch space between the two glass skins in which air circulates, allowing the bioclimatic functioning of the building.

The interiors of the building are arranged around this central space in a concentric pattern, in which four large structural columns, the stairs and elevators and the service areas are arranged symmetrically around a large central corridor, while the two outer bands of offices and work areas are positioned along the façade, in order to benefit from the natural light, thus reducing energy consumption yet further. Solar cells on the rooftop allow the building to be partially self-sufficient in terms of energy production.

The bioclimatic functioning of the tower does not depend on the large central space alone, but also on the 12-inch (30-cm) space between the two skins, in which air circulates to avoid overheating.

90-91 ■ The roof of the tower, with an inside view of the façade that continues above the roof of the building to create a dematerialized effect, in the foreground and the volume that houses a restaurant with panoramic views over the Rhine on the right.

90 bottom ■ This view from the ground of the roof that surrounds the base of the tower emphasizes its triangular shape.

The temperature of the air trapped between the two surfaces changes so that when it reaches the interiors it has already been heated or cooled in relation to the outside temperature.

Brises-soleils are housed between the two glazed surfaces and controlled by a computerized system, which adjusts their angle according to that of the sun, ensuring the optimal comfort of the interiors. They are mainly angled on the southern side and horizontal on the north, allowing the façades to function and be arranged in different ways.

In addition to the brises-soleils, the 12-inch (30-cm) space between the two layers of glass also houses an installation by French artist Yann Kersalé: a series of red, blue and yellow lights that, combined with the lighting of the interiors, enhances the stratified transparency of the façade and changes its color, giving the office building a highly innovative, playful, cheerful and ephemeral appearance.

8 CANADA SQUARE

[LONDON ■ UK]

The design of the HSBC Group's international headquarters (8 Canada Square) in London was entrusted to Norman Foster, who built its previous head office in Hong Kong in 1986 – an extraordinary hi-tech building characterized by the large suspension trusses on its façade, giving it a more complex image than its London counterpart. The latter is situated in the Canary Wharf complex, which was one of the earliest projects for the redevelopment of London's urban docklands into an important financial and banking district during the early 1990s. The master plan of the area occupied by the warehouses was entrusted to Skidmore, Owings & Merrill LLP, while Cesar Pelli designed the building that became the symbol of the development – Canary Wharf Tower – completed in 1991. Over the years a series of other skyscrapers have been built on the site, forming a new vertical landscape three miles from central London, to which it is linked by the efficient and rapid Docklands Light Railway, whose main station is located at the base of Pelli's tower.

The master plan was laid out like a checkerboard, with several green squares around which the headquarters of leading international companies were built. Canada Square is the site of the HSBC Tower and the Citigroup Centre, both designed by Norman Foster, and a building by Skidmore, Owings & Merrill LLP occupied by Bank of America and Crédit Suisse First Boston. Another tower by Cesar Pelli stands to the east. These skyscrapers form a group, characterized by regular forms and mainly clear glass façades. Standing 689 ft (210 m) high, with 48 stories (44 floors and 4 basements), the HSBC Group headquarters, completed in 2002, is second in height only to Canary Wharf Tower.

92 ■ At night the form of the tower is modified by the internal lighting, which dematerializes the volume and emphasizes the pattern of the stories.

93 ■ 8 Canada Square is a regular rectangular block with rounded corners encased by an elegant curtain wall that alternates clear glass with bands of white ceramic material.

94 bottom ■ Works of art adorn the lobby, beneath which a three-story private car park and a pedestrian underpass to the Canary Wharf subway station are situated.

The title of London's highest building and the prestige of the entire development is probably destined to change again over the next few years following the construction in the City of a series of skyscrapers, including the Pinnacle (or Bishopsgate Tower) by Kohn Pedersen Fox (945 ft/288 m), the Leadenhall Building by Richard Rogers (737 ft/225 m) and 30 St Mary Axe (or Swiss Re Tower, 590 ft/180 m) also by Norman Foster, which will draw the city's economic and financial district back to its original location.

The most distinctive characteristic of 8 Canada Square is its regular shape, which contrasts with the bizarre silhouettes of the skyscrapers of the City, for it is set in an area that is largely defined by the use of simple rectangular blocks.

Nonetheless, Foster's hallmark is apparent in several details the elegant and minimalist form is distinguished by its rounded corners and a façade that alternates clear glass with bands of white ceramic material, thus marking the stories of the tower

94-95 ■ The base of the tower is completely transparent, flooding the 92-foot-high lobby with light and allowing it to engage with the outside space of the square.

The base is completely transparent, connecting the outside space with the 92-ft (28-m) high lobby, where a multimedia installation recounts the company's history. This inner area allows access to the floors above – housing offices and 3 with meeting rooms, cafés and stores – and to those below street level, which are home to an underground railway station and a 3-story car park. The interiors are arranged around a central core and feature an open plan making them light and airy. The Building Research Establishment, the highest British authority in environmental standards, has pronounced Foster's tower an excellent building in terms of energy consumption (the elevators, for example, go into in standby mode when not in use), recycled materials and CO_2 emissions.

LOCATION	PROJECT	HEIGHT	FLOORS	YEAR
LONDON (UK)	FOSTER + PARTNERS	689 FT 210 M	48	2002

DENTSU HEADQUARTERS BUILDING

[TOKYO ▪ JAPAN]

French architect Jean Nouvel's designs have always been characterized by experimentation with the various effects of transparency, fading, and dematerialization that can be created with different materials and light. As Nouvel himself says, he is interested in the highly strategic relationship between light and matter in the development of architecture, for the use of certain materials allows a building to be programmed in different ways over time and the architect can play with ephemeral effects. Nouvel maintains that playing with transparency always means playing with matter alone to give a building different faces. He notes that glass allows the architect to manipulate depth, transparency in the strict sense of the word, chiaroscuro and much more besides, adding, "My buildings try to play with the effects of virtuality, appearance. Viewers wonder if the material is present or not. We create virtual images; we create ambiguity."

Nouvel's work is characterized by transparency, voids, reflections, fading and dematerialization, as testified by buildings ranging from the Arab World Institute to the Fondation Cartier and the Tour Sans Fins ("Tower without Ends") in Paris. His structures have always sought to surprise, intrigue and grab the attention with effects that destabilize our perception, confusing the boundaries between building and setting, architecture and nature. The tower that he recently built in Tokyo for the Dentsu advertising agency is no exception. However, like the Torre Agbar in Barcelona, the building combines the various devices that produce these effects in a formal arrangement

96 ▪ **The tower overlooks the Hamarikyu Gardens with which it engages through its curved form and glass skin formed of panels with varying degrees of transparency.**

97 ▪ **This view highlights the tower's plastic form: the volume is the result of the extrusion of a shape resembling a bird's wing or a crescent.**

98-99 ■ The large entrance hall is surrounded by glass walls. Glass elevators are positioned along the tower's straight side; their transparency allows their movement to create an impression of dynamic space both inside and outside the building.

LOCATION	PROJECT	HEIGHT	FLOORS	YEAR
TOKYO (JAPAN)	ATELIERS JEAN NOUVEL	700 FT 213 M	48	2002

99 ■ The tower's skin is characterized by varying degrees of transparency, shades of gray and reflective properties, giving it a constantly changing appearance.

that is completely lacking in his previous works, characterized by simple volumes or successions of stories.

The Dentsu Tower has a striking form, resembling a wing or a crescent, achieved by the extrusion of a triangular base whose rounded corners have different angles. Consequently, its appearance varies depending on viewpoint. The skin of the building also changes constantly according to the way in which the light hits it. This effect is achieved by the use of layers of screen-printed glass with varying degrees of transparency, shades of gray and reflective properties, and allows the façade to appear as continuous (it's difficult to distinguish the windows), but never static. This sets it apart from the neighboring buildings, characterized by the repetitive design of their openings and the largely regular arrangement of their volumes, which echo the urban grid plan above the ground, from which Nouvel's building is completely independent. The tower's aerodynamic silhouette allows it to engage with its setting in a different way: the most regular straight façade faces the city, while the slightly curved opposite side overlooks the Hamarikyu Gardens. This park is an additional reason for the choice of a transparent façade, which is able to engage with nature by reflecting it, like the Fondation Cartier in Paris.

The Dentsu Tower is part of a redevelopment scheme for an area formerly occupied by a railway station, situated between the Hamarikyu Gardens and Tokyo Bay. The form and materials chosen by the French architect have allowed the construction of a tower that engages with its setting, has a distinctive image, and offers great comfort to its occupants. Indeed, the reflective façade reduces solar transmission while allowing the penetration of natural light, thus optimizing energy consumption, which is further reduced by the presence of a series of terraced gardens at different heights, ensuring natural ventilation and the constant renewal of air.

The building's aerodynamic shape attenuates the impact of wind and earthquakes, which is absorbed by a steel structure positioned around its perimeter and inside the service core.

A large entrance hall occupies the entire base of the building and is also characterized by reflective and transparent effects from the outside. A series of glass elevators is positioned along the tower's straight side, their continuous movement is visible from both inside and outside the building creating an impression of dynamism and vitality.

ONE PEKING ROAD

[HONG KONG ■ THE PEOPLE'S REP. OF CHINA]

The imposing skyline of central Hong Kong's skyline rises on the side of Victoria Harbour opposite Kowloon, where the height of buildings was long restricted due to its proximity to the airport. Following the relocation of the airport to Lantau, the skyline of the area overlooking the bay started to be transformed with a series of new buildings, including One Peking Road, consisting of a long narrow rectangular block overlaid with a curved curtain wall on the southern side. It is situated close to the Former Marine Police Headquarters, a two-story colonial building that stands on a hill, against which the base of the tower is built. The connection between the two buildings – and between old and new – was one of the main themes tackled by the architect. The result is a dual connection: a visual one, created by constructing a totally transparent structure, and a physical one, established via the base of the tower, both at roof level (featuring a public garden) and inside, where a large foyer also allows access to the bus station situated on a lower level and linked by a system of escalators and subways. The old and new buildings thus offer the city an array of public areas and facilities. The former is now occupied by a tourist center, while the latter has 5 floors with many restaurants, 14 floors of offices and a further 3 floors of restaurants at the top, which offer spectacular views over the bay.

The northern façade of One Peking Road is formed by a skin composed of three layers of glass, allowing the air circulating between them to reduce solar transmission, while the curved southern façade is also made of glass, but shaded by horizontal aluminum brises-soleils. This shading system characterizes its design and enables the use of more transparent glass, thus allowing maximum natural light to penetrate the interiors.

100 ■ **The section of One Peking Road shows how it engages with both the hill against which it is built and the colonial building of the Former Marine Police Headquarters.**

101 ■ **The tower takes the form of a parallelepiped, whose short side overlooks the street, while the main façade covered by the curved wall engages with the hill.**

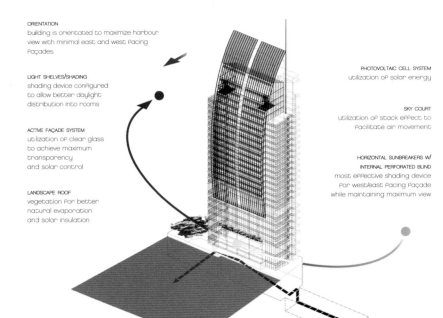

ORIENTATION
building is orientated to maximize harbour
view with minimal east and west facing
façades.

LIGHT SHELVES/SHADING
shading device configured
to allow better daylight
distribution into rooms

ACTIVE FAÇADE SYSTEM
utilization of clear glass
to achieve maximum
transparency
and solar control

LANDSCAPE ROOF
vegetation for better
natural evaporation
and solar insulation

PHOTOVOLTAIC CELL SYSTEM
utilization of solar energy

SKY COURT
utilization of stack effect to
facilitate air movement

HORIZONTAL SUNBREAKERS W/
INTERNAL PERFORATED BLIND
most effective shading device
for west/east facing façade
while maintaining maximum view

←→

102 top ■ The tower is equipped with systems to reduce energy consumption while ensuring maximum natural illumination and spectacular views.

103 ■ The profile of the short sides appears very slender, due to the extension of the curved surfaces above the top of the building and to the pattern of the façade that marks the floors.

The curved façade extends above the actual building, making the tower appear taller and slenderer than it actually is. As this part of the façade is not required to protect and illuminate the area behind it, it is used to house the solar panels that make the building almost completely self-sufficient in terms of energy production. The entire height of the east and west façades is fitted with louvers that change their position according to the intensity of the sun by means of automated sensors. Energy consumption is further reduced by the presence of a garden on the roof of the base, which lowers the temperature of the spaces inside it, and a sky court at the top of the tower, which aids the circulation of air.

Finally, the curved form of the façade allows wind loads to be reduced and makes the building appear slenderer. The structure of the tower is very simple, for it is composed of a reinforced concrete central core housing the circulation and service areas and positioned asymmetrically along the curved façade, and a row of hollow steel columns packed with concrete. The sail-shaped façade is thus the fundamental feature of the design, for it contributes to both its structural and bioclimatic functioning, while at the same time distinguishing the building with a form that gives it an original sculptural appearance and symbolizes its proximity to the sea. Indeed, although One Peking Road is unable to compete with the much taller buildings that characterize Hong Kong's central district, it immediately became the landmark in this part of the city.

←←

102 bottom ■ This detail of the curved façade shows the relationship between the transparent curtain wall and the brise-soleil system.

LOCATION	PROJECT	HEIGHT	FLOORS	YEAR
HONG KONG (THE PEOPLE'S REPUBLIC OF CHINA)	DESIGN ARCHITECT: ROCCO DESIGN ARCHITECTS LIMITED - ARCHITECT OF RECORD: WMKY LTD	525 FT 160 M	30	2003

30 ST MARY AXE

[LONDON ■ UK]

The new tower built by Norman Foster for leading insurance firm Swiss Re was the first of a series of skyscrapers whose bizarre silhouettes and forms are destined over the next few years to revolutionize the skyline of the City of London (as capital's historic financial center is called). The building is known as 30 St Mary Axe, or the Swiss Re Tower. The new towers will replace old buildings that stood on the site of the Baltic Exchange, a Victorian structure that was damaged by an IRA bomb and subsequently demolished. Its presence in an area that, while not on any of the sightlines and thus not subject to particular restrictions, did not witness the construction of any structures taller than the height of the dome of St Paul's Cathedral for many years indicates a change in attitude to the building of skyscrapers in the city's historic district. Although London is one of the European cities with the greatest number of towers (mainly medium/high, about 330 ft/100 m), the debate continues, owing also to the fact that there are various projects in the works, of which Foster is the most prominent supporter.

The urban setting of 30 St Mary Axe is well within the city's main financial district. The tower is situated opposite Holland House, the only building by Hendrik Petrus Berlage in London, and the Aviva Tower, an International Style block built during the 1960s, not far from the Lloyd's Building by Richard Rogers. The other structures surrounding it are largely medium/tall buildings with regular shapes. In this fairly homogeneous urban landscape, the tower's iconic figure – which has been likened to a gherkin, a pinecone, a bullet and many other images – makes it a distinctive feature

104 ■ **The tower's skin is formed by a double layer of glass encasing a steel grid; both surfaces are defined by a diamond pattern.**

105 ■ **This view of the City from the southern bank of the Thames shows how the skyline has changed since the construction of Foster's tower.**

→→

106 top ■ This photograph shows a detail of the top of the tower during its construction.

of the London skyline. It has paved the way for the worldwide diffusion of singular sky-scrapers with bizarre shapes, "architecture without the form of buildings," outsized and strangely shaped in relation to the surrounding constructions. Indeed, this trend is set to transform the City of London over the coming years, populating its urban landscape with singular silhouettes, ranging from the spiral of the Pinnacle by Kohn Pedersen Fox to the pointed Leadenhall Building by Richard Rogers and the Shard by Renzo Piano.

The form of Foster's tower, which rises from a circular base, bulging out slightly to reach its maximum width about halfway up, before tapering to a domed tip, was the result of the architect's two-fold desire to create a singular sculptural object and to satisfy certain environmental requirements, allowing the building to function for 40 percent of the year without resorting to sophisticated ventilation and cooling systems. It thus continues the quest that Foster commenced with the Commerzbank Tower in Frankfurt, which develops ideas first explored in the Climatroffice, an office building enclosed in a "shape-less" glass skin designed in the 1970s by Richard Buckminster Fuller. The Commerzbank Tower is a bioclimatic building, due to a sequence of empty spaces and sky gardens that form a hollow spiral within it and a large central light well, which together allow the formation of updrafts.

This mechanism is repeated and refined in the London building, in which the floor plan of each level has a circular perimeter indented by six triangular light courts. The floor plan is rotated for each successive floor, creating hollow spirals that allow

←→

106 bottom ■ The section shows the hollow spirals created by the gaps in each floor. Air and light circulate in these shafts, allowing energy consumption to be reduced.

107 ■ The shape of the tower is based on a circular plan that bulges outwards until about halfway up the tower, before tapering to the domed top.

LOCATION	PROJECT	HEIGHT	FLOORS	YEAR
LONDON (UK)	FOSTER + PARTNERS	590 FT 180 M	42	2003

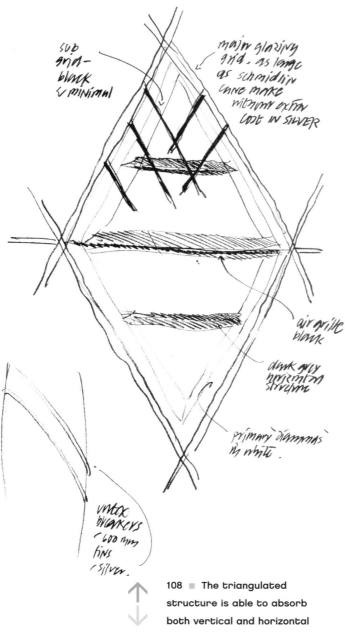

sub grid – black & minimal

major glazing grid. as large as schmidlin can make without extra cost in silver

air grille black

dark grey horizontal structure

primary diagrams in white.

vortex breakers ~ 600 mm fins ~ silver.

108 ■ The triangulated structure is able to absorb both vertical and horizontal loads, permitting a substantial reduction in the amount of steel required for the frame.

108-109 ■ Despite the diagrid around the tower's perimeter, its interiors are very well lit and offer spectacular views of the City.

updrafts and the diffusion of natural light between stories, greatly reducing the energy consumption of the air-conditioning and lighting systems. However, the spiral is not simply a hollow space for the circulation of air and light, but the geometric figure that characterizes the entire building and determines the relationship between section and elevation and between the tower's structural skin and its contents. Indeed, the skin is characterized by a structural frame of steel lozenges that envelops the building's conical form and is double glazed. This diagrid absorbs both vertical and horizontal forces, obviating the need for wind-bracing structures and allowing the thickness of the walls to be reduced. The layered composition of the skin and inner screen allows the circulation of air, while the use of reflective glass cause the appearance of the tower to change constantly, due to the effects of transparency and reflection. The building's aerodynamic shape not only promotes the circulation of air inside, but also avoids interference with the air currents, which are interrupted and channeled towards the ground floor in International Style rectangular blocks.

The tower's slender form reduces refraction, thus increasing the amount of light that reaches the interiors. The fact that its circumference is narrower at the base allows part of the area of the plot to be freed for the creation of a plaza that connects the street to the foyer and public floors of the building. The stories around the

110-111 ■ The top floor houses a restaurant ======sting 360-degree views over the City.

111 top ■ The plan of the structure shows how the diagrid defines the entire volume up to the very top, ending in the circular shape that houses the lens-shaped piece of glass.

base are home to stores and cafés, while the floor beneath the glass dome at the top of the tower houses a restaurant with spectacular 360-degree views of the City. Finally, the intermediate floors house the offices and work areas for the employees of the Swiss Re insurance company.

111 bottom ■ The dome at the top of the tower is completely glazed and is capped by a lens-shaped piece of glass.

HIGHCLIFF

[HONG KONG ■ THE PEOPLE'S REPUBLIC OF CHINA]

Highcliff in Hong Kong is one of the world's highest residential buildings. It is remarkably slim for such a tall structure, as the local scarcity of building sites meant that architect Dennis Lau was faced with the challenge of achieving high residential density with minimal ground space. However, this was not the only problem that he had to solve, for the sloping site and the presence of strong winds and typhoons further complicated the construction of such a large building.

The tower is situated high on the east side of Victoria Peak, in a position that is exposed to winds, but is also highly visible, allowing the apartments that it houses to enjoy extraordinary views. Consequently, Lau chose a form derived from the extrusion of two intersecting ellipses. This curved, aerodynamic shape allowed him to achieve an original structure, reminiscent of Philip Johnson's Lipstick Building in New York, while mitigating the effect of the wind.

On the floor plan the structural core and the circulation areas are housed where the two ellipses intersect, allowing the entire space along the façade to be divided

← →

112 ■ Highcliff's slender 831-foot silhouette dominates Victoria Harbour from the slopes of Victoria Peak.

113 ■ The tower's sinuous form is emphasized by its curtain wall, whose design alternates steel bands, marking the floors, with reflective glass panels.

114 ■ Highcliff's base rests on a seven-story podium that anchors it to the slope and connects it to the Summit, a neighboring residential tower.

115 bottom ■ The swimming pool housed in the podium is also elliptical in shape and is lavishly decorated with a mosaic that continues the striking theme of the lobby mural.

LOCATION	PROJECT	HEIGHT	FLOORS	YEAR
HONG KONG (THE PEOPLE'S REPUBLIC OF CHINA)	DENNIS LAU & NG CHUN MAN ARCHITECTS & ENGINEERS (HK) LTD	831.36 FT 253.4 M	73	2003

115 top ■ The general plan of the podium shows gardens, a large swimming pool and a ramp leading to the underground car park outside the huge lobby.

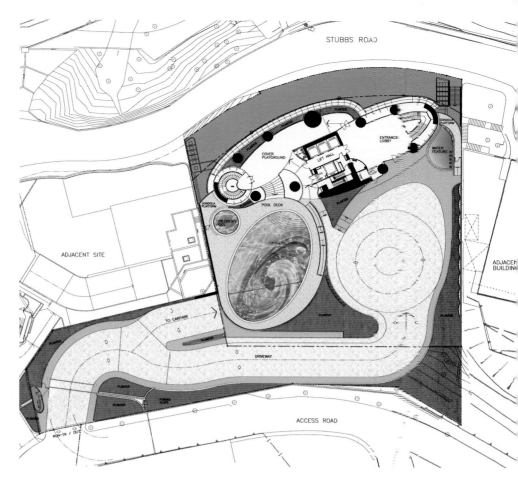

to two large apartments with splendid views. As in other residential buildings with similar proportions (e.g., Costas Kondylis' Trump World Tower in New York) the interiors are lavishly finished and decorated, as they are destined for particularly wealthy occupants. The base of the tower rests on a seven-story podium that fulfils the dual function of anchoring it to the slope by extending its area and housing a series of luxury facilities, including a car park, a swimming pool and exclusive clubs for the demanding residents.

The elegance of the building is also expressed in the design of the curtain wall which is divided horizontally with each floor marked by a steel band topped by reflecting glass. This arrangement recalls that adopted by Cesar Pelli for the Petronas Twin Towers, where it is made even more grandiose by the historicizing form of the building and the golden color of the steel.

The decision to give Highcliff's façade a horizontal design, instead of an unbroken one such as that used for the Trump World Tower, was motivated by the desire to play down its overly accentuated vertical dimension, while associating it with an iconography closer to traditional Oriental buildings.

The design choices regarding the tower's formal aspects and circulation areas coincide with the structural ones: the plan based on two ellipses – devised to avoid creating hierarchies between the façades, occupied exclusively by the residential units – required a reinforced concrete structural core housing the circulation areas to be situated at their meeting point and a series of columns to be positioned around them

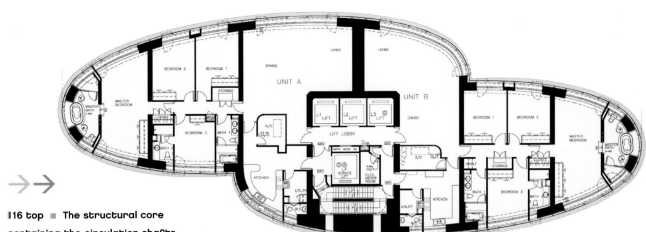

116 top ■ The structural core containing the circulation shafts is housed in the area where the two ellipses intersect, allowing the residential units to be arranged along the façades.

These two systems are connected and reinforced by a series of concrete dividing walls and external trusses. The connecting walls between the outer columns and the central core divide the interiors with rigorous orthogonal lines, betraying the dynamic arrangement of the exterior. The tower is completed by a wind damper system on the roof, which minimizes the building's movements.

116 bottom ■ The large lobby echoes the curved lines of the façade and can be accessed via an uplit glass staircase.

117 ■ The tower's interiors are painstakingly finished and decorated, for the apartments are destined for particularly wealthy occupants.

TWO INTERNATIONAL FINANCE CENTRE

[HONG KONG ■ THE PEOPLE'S REPUBLIC OF CHINA]

Hong Kong boasts one of the world's most beautiful skylines, in terms of both its natural features – it is enclosed by the Peak on one side and Victoria Harbour on the other – and its wealth of bizarre, abstract, traditional and technological silhouettes created by leading international architects. These include the HSBC Main Building by Norman Foster, the Bank of China Tower by Ieoh M. Pei, the Cheung Kong Center by Cesar Pelli, The Center by Dennis Lau, and Two International Finance Centre by Cesar Pelli. The American architect's design for the latter won the competition held by the Mass Transit Railway Corporation and Central Waterfront Property Project Development Limited because it revives the archetypal image of the skyscraper, symbolizing the role that this building type has always played in the collective imagination. Indeed, it takes the form of an obelisk soaring toward the sky, whose height of 1378 ft (420 m) makes it a giant when compared to the city and the port, allowing it to embody Hong Kong's international role.

The competition did not merely call for an office tower that related to the city through its iconic silhouette, but also required a vast complex, featuring a second 38-story tower housing a hotel and apartments, a new railway terminus connected to the ferry terminal and the airport, and a basement with a 4-story shopping mall and a garden roof. The aim was to create a piece of city with a cluster of functions and spaces – public and private – and a hub for the various infrastructure and transport networks

118-119 ■ **The Hong Kong skyline is one of the most varied in the world in terms of its geometric shapes. It is dominated by Two International Finance Centre, a 1378-foot-tall tower by Cesar Pelli.**

119 ■ **The verticality of the tower, which Pelli describes as a skyscraper's principal feature, is heightened when viewed from below and underscored by the pattern formed by the uprights of its façade.**

allowing access to the island. This role is also confirmed by the image of a sort of gate or monumental entrance to the city created by Two International Finance Centre and the International Commerce Center on the opposite side of the bay. The building's task of access point and international traffic hub is aided by its position on a drained site, which has allowed space to be created on the otherwise densely packed waterfront, thus making it the first landmark visible when arriving by sea.

Owing to the building's strategic and symbolic role, Pelli decided to use a familiar formula: the combination of historical forms with advanced technologies, in order to ensure that the image satisfied the necessary requirements for a skyscraper that, according to the architect, must be founded on "a centric form [that] tapers with well-proportioned setbacks, expressing a vertical ascending movement." Consequently, the architect chose the most iconic figure of this architectural type, as embodied by the early American skyscrapers with their Art Deco language, rather than a form drawn from the local culture and architectural tradition, as he did for the Petronas Twin Towers. Two International Finance Centre

LOCATION	PROJECT	HEIGHT	FLOORS	YEAR
HONG KONG (THE PEOPLE'S REPUBLIC OF CHINA)	DESIGN ARCHITECT: PELLI CLARKE PELLI ARCHITECTS ASSOCIATE ARCHITECT: ADAMSON ASSOCIATES ARCHITECT OF RECORD: ROCCO DESIGN LIMITED	1378 FT 420 M	88	2004

120-121 ■ The lobby at the base of the tower is surrounded by glass walls, in order to engage its interior with the exterior.

121 ■ This picture shows the entire building, with its characteristic rounded corners and successive setbacks.

thus appears as a tower with stepped-in corners and a stepped-back profile that narrows toward the summit, which is defined by an original crown composed of narrow claws recalling those of Pelli's Bank of America Corporate Center in Charlotte, North Carolina. The architect has also replicated the illumination of the latter, which emphasizes the tower's structure and summit and creates spectacular effects at night that allow Two International Finance Centre to compete with the other giants of the Hong Kong skyline.

Pelli maintains that the main task of a skyscraper is to soar upward to express the maximum possible verticality, and this feature is underscored not only by the graceful crown, but also by the materials used for the building's cladding: a curtain wall of reflecting glass supported by silver-colored steel uprights, whose design further emphasizes the skyward thrust.

The height of the building (1378 ft/420 m) is made possible by an external structure of hollow steel mega-columns packed with concrete, and a reinforced concrete central core that houses the circulation and service areas. The columns are connected to the core at 20-story intervals by steel trusses that reinforce the structure to enable it to withstand the impact of the frequent typhoons that strike Hong Kong.

TORRE AGBAR

[BARCELONA ■ SPAIN]

The 474-ft (142-m) tall Torre Agbar has redesigned the Barcelona skyline, rising above a predominantly horizontal cityscape, with the exception of Montserrat, the Sagrada Família and Montjuïc, with which the tower establishes a dialogue. Owing to its site in Plaça de les Glòries Catalanes, the meeting point of the city's main thoroughfares – Avinguda Diagonal, Avinguda Meridiana and Gran Via de les Corts Catalanes – the tower is immediately visible both to those traveling along these streets and to those arriving in Barcelona by air or by sea.

The Torre Agbar is the first stage in an extensive redevelopment scheme that aims to transform the district of Sant Martí into a business and technological city, of which it is the symbol. Following its construction in 2004, the building was an immediate success, becoming an icon of Barcelona itself. Its unusual shape, resembling a bullet or a gherkin, similar to Norman Foster's 30 St Mary Axe in London, makes the tower immediately recognizable on the Barcelona skyline, just like Foster's building in the British capital. However, architect Jean Nouvel claims that he drew his inspiration from the mountains of Montserrat, the architecture of Gaudí and Catalan culture, noting that such a structure could only have been built in Barcelona: "This is not a tower, a skyscraper, in the American sense. It is a unique emergence, rising singularly in the center of a generally calm city. Unlike the slender spires and bell towers that typically pierce the horizons of horizontal cities, this tower is a fluid mass that bursts through the ground like a geyser under permanent, calculated pressure. The surface of the building evokes water: smooth and continuous, shimmering and transparent, its

← →

122 ■ The unusual silhouette of the 474-foot-tall Torre Agbar is a distinctive feature on the city's skyline.

123 ■ The tower is one of the first examples with a singular shape, quite unlike that of traditional skyscrapers and modeled instead on natural forms like pinecones or geysers.

124 bottom ■ This detail of the façade shows the sequence of layers: the inner structural concrete skin, the intermediate layer of colored panels and the outer one consisting of a glass brise-soleil.

materials reveal themselves in nuanced shades of color and light."

As in many of Nouvel's other works, the design process is born out of the fusion of several specific features of the site: the characteristics of the setting and the forms present in it, but also the local restrictions, regulations, technical and functional requirements that a building must comply with and satisfy, along with the architect's sensitivity and personal quest.

LOCATION	PROJECT	HEIGHT	FLOORS	YEAR
BARCELONA (SPAIN)	ATELIERS JEAN NOUVEL - B720 ARQUITECTURA S.L.	474 FT 142 M	33	2004

124-125 ■ As in many of Jean Nouvel's other works, the Torre Agbar creates effects of transparency and dematerialization, achieved with its multi-layer structural skin.

That of Nouvel probes the relationships between matter and perception, seeking depth through a succession of surface layers, many of which are transparent. The resulting visual effects suggest the dematerialization and dissolution of volumes, which change according to the light.

In the Barcelona building these effects – intended to evoke the image of a geyser and smooth, transparent water – are achieved by means of a series of layers: an inner structural concrete skin, an intermediate layer of colored panels and an outer one consisting of a glass brise-soleil. Together they create a pixelated image that changes continuously due to the transparent and reflective effects and plays of light and shade produced by the various layers. The inner concrete skin is perforated by 4400 irregularly placed windows. Although their position and size may appear random, they are actually determined by the level of solar radiation and views over the city. For example, those facing the Sagrada Familia are larger. This concrete layer is covered with colored panels in 40 different colors, ranging from red to grey, blue and green. The warmer colors are positioned at the base of the tower and the cooler ones at the top. The outermost layer is composed of a glass brise-soleil system, whose louvers are oriented on the basis of the building's exposure to the sun and adjusted automatically by sensors according to the outside temperature. This series of layers not only defines the image of the

126-127 ■ An inside view of the glass and steel dome on top of the tower.

126 bottom ■ Viewed from the inside of the tower, the façade is distinguished by holes in its structural concrete skin. While their location and size may appear random, they are actually determined by the level of solar radiation and views over the city.

tower, but also creates a sort of thermal shield that protects the building from cold in winter and heat in summer.

The structure of the tower consists of two cylindrical volumes, both made from reinforced concrete: an asymmetrically positioned inner core housing the circulation areas and an outer skin that defines the volume of the building. The absence of other structural elements leaves the spaces between them free, allowing them to be arranged as wished. While the inner core extends as far as the 31st story, the outer skin reaches only to the 26th, and the upper 5 stories are set in the central core and covered with a glass dome. This too is composed of two layers: an inner one of transparent panels, which assume various shades of blue in order to continue the pixelated effect of the tower, and an external one constituted by glass brisessoleils. The tower thus gradually dematerializes towards the top, offering the same effect proposed for the Tour Sans Fins in the Parisian district of La Défense.

A cutaway view of the tower reveals four segments with a technical floor between each. The top segment contains the management offices and meeting rooms, while the two middle segments house eight floors of offices and the cafeteria. The bottom segment is more complex, featuring a large double-height entrance hall on street level with a floor for medical services and four floors of offices above. Below ground it houses a four-story car park, an auditorium and a plant room.

127 bottom ■ The large entrance hall is defined by the light that filters through the irregular holes in the skin and the primary colors that characterize both the walls and the furnishings.

128 bottom ■ This nighttime view of the base of the tower shows the ramp that allows access to the lower floors, in the foreground, and the brise-soleil system covering the façade.

← ←

128-129 and 129 bottom ■ The Torre Agbar is illuminated at night, further reinforcing the pixelated image of its façade. The graduated colors – red at the base, blue towards the top – make it a distinctive landmark visible from afar.

←↑

TAIPEI 101

[TAIPEI - TAIWAN ■ THE REPUBLIC OF CHINA]

Rising 1671 ft (509 m), Taipei 101 – named after its location and number of stories – displaced Kuala Lumpur's Petronas Twin Towers (1483 ft/452 m) as the world's tallest building. However, in the endless battle for the record, the Taipei skyscraper has already been overtaken by the Burj Dubai, currently under construction, which will stand 2684 feet (818 m) tall, with 162 stories, when completed. Taipei 101 is the new landmark of Taiwan's capital city and the symbol of the economic growth, international prestige and extraordinary technical expertise of a small country able to build such a tall tower in a highly seismic area with sandy soil and frequent high winds and typhoons. This challenge required not only advanced technologies and skilled workers, but also a new iconography deeply rooted in local tradition.

While in Western cities, power is represented by innovative, bizarre images that aim to astonish, in the Far East it is replaced by forms evoking elements, architecture, theories and philosophies closely associated with the local culture with which the inhabitants can immediately identify. Well aware of this, Cesar Pelli featured the forms of

← →

130 ■ The tower's immediately recognizable form fits in well with its urban setting: it clearly belongs to the local culture, yet its giant scale allows it to engage with the global landscape.

131 ■ The structure of the building evokes that of a bamboo shoot, for it is composed of a series of segments, each of which rises out of the previous one. Its shape is defined by sloping walls formed by a double layer of green heat-absorbing glass.

LOCATION	PROJECT	HEIGHT	FLOORS	YEAR
TAIPEI - TAIWAN (THE REPUBLIC OF CHINA)	C.Y. LEE & PARTNERS	1671 FT 509 M	101	2004

the minaret and the pagoda in his Petronas Towers. Similarly, the pagoda also inspired Skidmore, Owings & Merrill's Jin Mao Building in Shanghai. For Taipei 101 C. Y. Lee – the Chinese-born architect also responsible for the Tuntex Sky Tower, whose form clearly betrays its local inspiration – chose a design combining elements of the pagoda and the traditional courtyard temple. The building recalls the traditional bamboo construction composed of various parts, each built on that below, thus revealing the influence of the philosophical theory of *yin* and *yang* and those derived from the *Yijing* or the "Book of Changes."

The entire design revolves around the number eight, which is a symbol of good luck, with the tower composed of eight segments, each having eight stories.

Each section is clad with inward-sloping walls, recalling a bamboo shoot, which is a symbol of prosperity and progress. This image is echoed in the structural design of the building, featuring a series of repeated segments, each of which is connected to and rises out of the previous one. Like the Jin Mao Building, Taipei 101 may be defined a "technological pagoda," for it combines traditional Chinese elements and symbols with the most advanced structural and engineering technologies. Indeed, the building holds the record for the world's fastest elevators, which move at a speed of 3307 ft (1008 m) per minute, thus reaching the roof, where a panoramic cabin is located, in just 39 seconds.

The use of advanced technologies characterizes both the structural elements of the building and its energy-saving and functional systems. As the tower needs to withstand both vertical loads and sideways pressure from earthquakes and typhoons, it has a central core with 16 huge box-shaped steel columns packed with reinforced concrete and a further eight mega-columns around the perimeter, which are connected to the core by outrigger trusses

132-133 and 133 ■ Traditional Chinese motifs not only define the tower's image, but also that of a series of decorative elements situated in various points of the building.

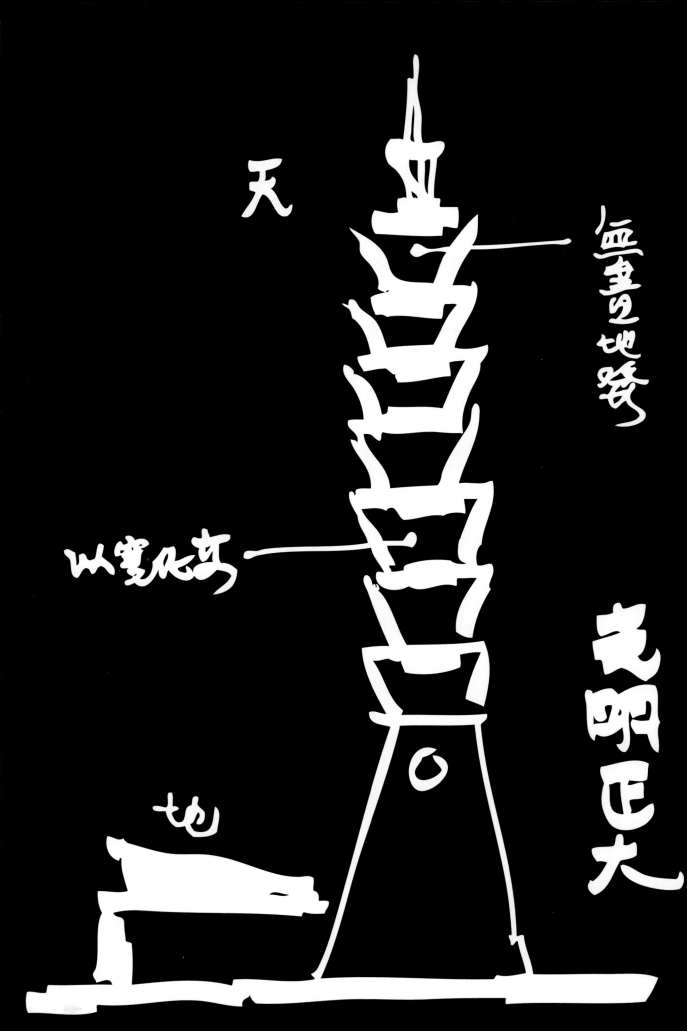

天

無量地聳

以雲化高

光明正大

也

正明

134 and 135 top ■ The design sketches show the various figures proposed for the tower, including a pagoda, all associated with the local tradition.

135 bottom ■ Other sketches show the studies for the possible arrangements of the circulation shafts.

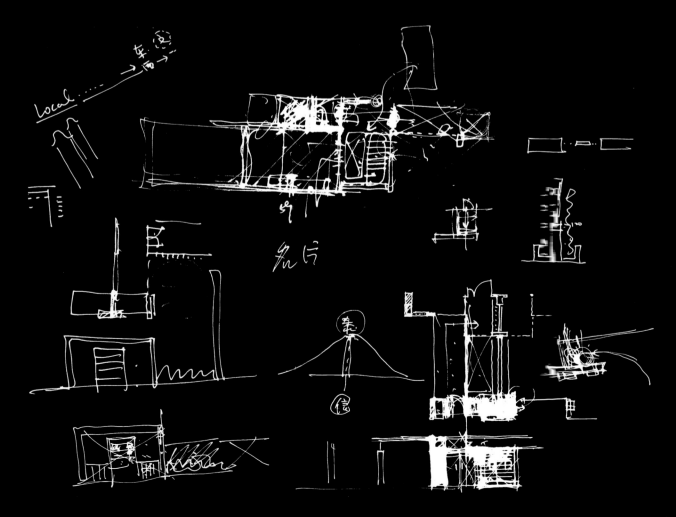

136-137 ■ The shopping mall in the base is arranged around a large central space crossed by monumental escalators.

136 bottom ■ This picture shows the cavity housing the pendulum, suspended from huge steel cables.

every eight floors. An 800-ton pendulum suspended from the 92nd floor stabilizes the upper part of the tower in the case of strong winds or earthquakes. The tower's curtain walls are double-glazed with heat-absorbing glass that allows the temperature to be controlled while permitting natural lighting of the interiors and ensuring good visibility. This cladding gives a uniform appearance to the various parts of the structure: a tall base housing a large atrium, shopping mall and fitness center; the eight segments housing offices and apartments; and the spire, around which a series of panoramic restaurants are clustered. Decorative features inspired by traditional Chinese motifs and figures characterize each of the sections.

At night Taipei 101 takes on a different appearance, for its illumination emphasizes the division of its segments and marks its floors, making it seem more fragmented but equally imposing on a skyline with no other buildings of similar monumental dimensions.

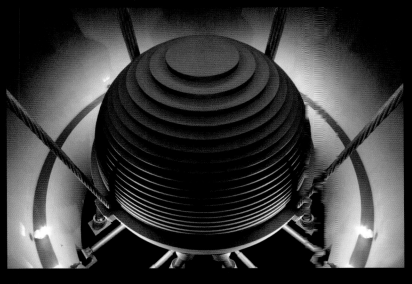

← ← 138-139 ■ These areas and the steel and glass roof covering them are gargantuan in scale.

↑ ↑ 139 top ■ The 800-ton pendulum, which stabilize the upper part of the tower in the case of strong winds or earthquakes, is suspended from the 92nd floor, almost at the top of the building.

139 bottom ■ A sort of capital with traditional Chinese motifs is featured between the columns and the huge skylight covering the public areas in the base.

MONTEVIDEO TOWER

[ROTTERDAM ■ THE NETHERLANDS]

Together with Norman Foster's World Port Center and Renzo Piano's KPN Telecom Building, the Montevideo Tower is one of the skyscrapers that have revolutionized the Rotterdam skyline. The 499-ft (152-m) tall building designed by the Mecanoo architecture firm stands on historic Wilhelmina Pier on the New Meuse River (a branch of the Rhine), from which the transatlantic liners once sailed for America. However, the area was largely abandoned following the construction of the city's new port closer to the sea.

In 1999 a redevelopment plan was drawn up for the entire area of Wilhelmina Pier. The southern part of the zone was entrusted to Mecanoo, with the aim of impressing global structure and identity on an area that was being developed only piecemeal, as exemplified by the office towers designed by Piano and Foster.

The scheme devised by Mecanoo allows these buildings to be integrated with a system of residential towers to form a vertical city, of which the Montevideo Tower is a sort of prototype. It is formed by a two-story rectangular base, whose steel frame is covered with a transparent skin that makes it permeable and open to the street. The base allows access to the three volumes that rise above it: the 499-ft (152-m) tall tower to the west; the Water Apartments, a 9-story building overhanging the base by 52 ft (15.8 m) to the northeast; and a 5-story block containing offices, restaurants, a swimming pool and a gym in the middle. The latter has fairly regular façades, marked by rectangular windows, like three of the façades of the Water Apartments. However, the southeast façade of the latter is characterized by rows of open galleries overlooking the waterfront.

The tower is more complex, for its façades are arranged as a series of volumes of different shapes, materials and colors, which appear to overlap and be set into each other. Some of them jut out towards the bay, while others seem to recede, although they are actually carved out of an array of terraces, open galleries and balconies, from which views of

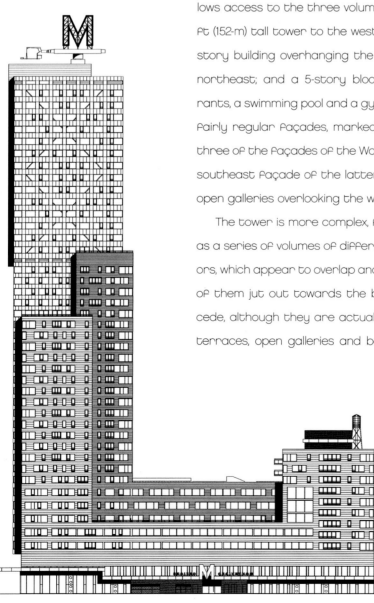

←→

140 ■ The elevation shows the base with the three superimposed volumes: the tower (west), the Water Apartments (northeast) and a building with offices, restaurants, swimming pool and gym in the middle.

141 ■ The Millennium Tower stands on Wilhelmina Pier, Rotterdam's historic gateway to the Rhine. At 499 ft (152 m) tall it has revolutionized the skyline of this part of the city.

← →

142 top ■ The Water Apartments building, in the foreground, is characterized by a single material with regular openings.

142-143 ■ The tower's façades feature volumes of different shapes, materials and colors. Some of these project towards the bay, while others are carved out of terraces, open galleries and balconies, boasting views of both the city centre and the sea.

both the city center and the sea can be admired, due to the virtual lack of tall buildings to the north. The articulation and differentiation of the elevations and parts was necessary to give the residential units a strong identity, removing them as far as possible from the serial image of traditional housing projects.

The wealth of materials, colors and spaces that characterizes the exterior image of the Montevideo Tower is echoed in the layout of its interiors. Indeed, the tower houses 192 residential units, divided into 54 different types with different floor areas and heights, allowing a huge variety of different plans and sections. The only element that remains constant is the central core housing the stairs and elevators. This type of layout with floors of different heights, open galleries and terraces evokes the transatlantic liners that once sailed from Rotterdam to America, and also the American skyscrapers of the 1950s and '60s, which are similarly characterized by galleries and terraces and the use of brick.

The structure of the Montevideo Tower also changes from level to level, alternating steel and concrete: the first 2 levels of the base are made from steel, the successive 27 floors from reinforced concrete, while steel is used again from the 28th floor upward, making the areas of the apartments more flexible and easily modifiable according to the requirements of their occupants.

142 bottom ■ The base that unites the various parts of the complex is covered with a transparent skin that makes it permeable and open to the street.

LOCATION	PROJECT	HEIGHT	FLOORS	YEAR
ROTTERDAM (THE NETHERLANDS)	MECANOO ARCHITECTEN	499 FT 152 M	43	2005

144-145 ■ The large columns that support the overhanging volume of the Water Apartments are also a feature of the building's interiors.

144 bottom ■ Long bands of windows flood the swimming pool in the middle building with natural light and offer spectacular views over the bay.

←←

145 bottom ■ The large glazed areas of the towers façades ensure that the residential units are also very well lit and allow them to enjoy breathtaking views over the surrounding area.

HSB
TURNING
TORSO
TOWER

[MALMÖ ■ SWEDEN]

→→

146 ■ This sketch clearly
shows the intention to convey
the concept of torsion with
a movement resembling that
of a twisting human torso.

The dynamic sculptural form of Santiago Calatrava's HSB Turning Torso Tower dominates the Malmö skyline. The tower, inspired by the movement of a twisting human body, is the tallest residential building in Sweden (623 ft/190 m high) and the second tallest in Europe. It is situated near the Oresund Bridge, linking Sweden and Denmark, and is the symbol of the redevelopment of the Western Harbor, an abandoned industrial area, and its transformation into a wealthy district overlooking the sea with residential units, offices and leisure facilities.

Following the construction of the Oresund Bridge, the entire city of Malmö has undergone great change and rapid population growth, prompting the local government to promote Sweden's first international housing exhibition in 2001. Participants were required to present a housing project that was both innovative in appearance and congruous with the Nordic landscape, while reconciling the use of advanced technologies with environmental awareness.

Santiago Calatrava was invited to design a residential tower in the Western Harbor area. The Spanish architect, who generally draws the inspiration for his work from the world of nature, had long been working on sculptures composed of a series of cubes, placed on top of each other and rotated, staggered, secured and supported by an external structure (such as those on which his recent design for a tower in New York is based).

The form of the Malmö tower is modeled on one of these sculptures, in which the cubes are progressively rotated to represent the effect of torsion. Indeed, Turning Torso is composed of nine identical cubes stacked one above the other and set in a central core of reinforced concrete, around which each is rotated by several degrees until reaching a total rotation of 90 degrees at the top of the tower. All of these segments are deformed on the side on which they are connected to a steel

147 ■ The profile of the tower, constituted by nine stacked cubes arranged around a central core, is most evident at dusk, when its internal lighting emphasizes the division of its parts. →→

exoskeleton – by means of a system of horizontal and diagonal bars and struts – that constitutes the tower's external spine and allows its torsion.

Each cube is an independent five-story building, detached from the one above it, and the intermediate space created between the blocks is used to house the technical equipment; each cube is also enclosed in a façade of aluminum and glass panels, characterized by a regular pattern of openings. The first 2 cubes contain 10 stories of offices, served by 2 elevators housed in the central core, while the successive 7 cubes contain 147 apartments with areas varying from 484 to 2045 sq. ft (45 to 190 sq. m). Each story has 5 apartments and the services are arranged around the central core, accessed by 3 elevators, allowing the main areas to be arranged along the façade, offering splendid views. The 53rd and 54th stories house a conference center, with views of Copenhagen to the west, Falsterbo to the south, the Scanian plain to the east and Helsinborg to the north.

The tower's innovativeness is not restricted to its dynamic form, but it also regards its construction technique. The reinforced concrete central core was the first element to be built and was used as a structural skeleton. Subsequently, the floors were constructed then the prefabricated residential units were added and connected to the external steel framework.

Like all the greatest high-tech architects, Calatrava manages to make the structure the main expressive medium of his work. Despite its traditionally solid and static nature, particularly in the case of high-rise buildings, he makes it extremely plastic and dynamic, closer to the organic natural world by which he is inspired than to the hyper-technological one of his peers.

LOCATION	PROJECT	HEIGHT	FLOORS	YEAR
MALMÖ (SWEDEN)	SANTIAGO CALATRAVA	623 FT 190 M	54	2005

148-149 ■ The regular pattern of the openings and the aluminum panels defines the façades of the cubes that compose the tower.

←→

150 ■ This detail of the façade, clad with aluminum panels, reveals the system of steel bars and struts connecting each cube.

151 top ■ A detail of the system of bars and struts that forms a sort of exoskeleton.

←←

151 center ■ A view of the intermediate spaces between the cubes.

←←

151 bottom ■ The large glazed surfaces ensure that the residential units are well lit and enjoy panoramic views.

151 HSB TURNING TORSO TOWER

152-153 ■ Each cube is deformed on the side on which it is connected to the steel exoskeleton via a system of bars and struts.

↑
↑

152 bottom and 153 bottom ■
The tower's exoskeleton is a sort
of external spine, which allows
its torsion.

←→

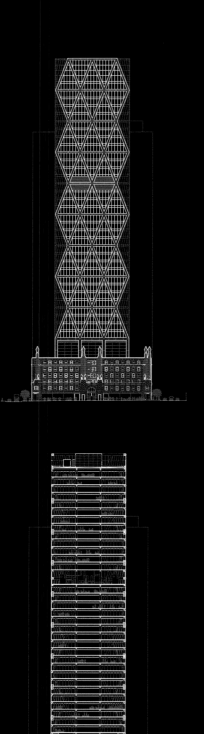

154 ■ The elevation and section of Norman Foster's tower reveals how it engages with the existing base by contrast; rising out of it while remaining detached from it.

HEARST TOWER

[NEW YORK ■ USA]

The new headquarters of the Hearst Corporation is a 597-ft (182-m) tower designed by British architect Norman Foster and characterized by a metal diagrid on a glass façade, rising out of a "historic" base: the six-story Hearst Magazine Building, built by architect Joseph Urban in 1928 and a designated landmark since 1988.

Once again Foster found himself dealing with a building of great historic and symbolic significance, as he had during the restoration of the Reichstag in Berlin and the redevelopment of the Great Court of the British Museum. In this case, he decided to build a completely new independent structure on top of the old one, entrusting the image of the tower to the use of advanced technology and materials – steel and glass – that contrast with the existing building. This takes the form of the Art Deco-style base of a tower that was never built, situated between 8th Avenue and 57th Street.

Its first two floors are marked by two grand entrances and large windows, while the successive four stories are characterized by the regular pattern of the windows and the enormous columns topped by statues that flank the entrances and adorn the chamfered corners of the regular volume. Foster did not alter its exterior, but hollowed out the building to create a huge inner space crossed by three large escalators surrounded by waterfalls and elevators that link the street-level lobby, with its cafés, restaurants and exhibition areas, to the office floors in the tower.

The area is flooded with light, for the new tower is set in the existing structure, but detached from it, with the space between the two volumes covered by a glass roof. Additionally, the first floor of the tower is positioned higher than the roof of the base and this vertical distance allows the height of its central part to be raised yet further. The tower is a parallelepiped with chamfered

155 ■ Foster's tower differs from the surrounding ones due to the metal diagrid enclosing its glass façade, which characterizes its outward appearance.

corners, like those of the base. However, it has a completely new image, due to the stainless steel structural diagrid and reflective glass façade. These elements give it a singular appearance, differentiating it from all the surrounding buildings, and the faceted corners in particular make its figure irregular, creating countless reflections.

The choice to use a structural diagrid instead of the commoner system of beams and columns allowed the thickness of the structural elements to be substantially reduced and avoided the need for wind-bracing structures. The entire building thus appears much lighter and greater permeability is possible between the inside and the outside. Finally, it was possible to keep the space inside the old building forming the tower's base completely free and unbroken, except for the vertical and diagonal supporting elements.

This building, like many others designed by Foster, has been planned to reduce energy consumption. Its structure is made from recycled steel; the masonry parts reuse the materials recovered from the demolition of the existing building; the glass façade is composed of panels with a coating that admits visible light

LOCATION	PROJECT	HEIGHT	FLOORS	YEAR
NEW YORK (USA)	FOSTER + PARTNERS - ADAMSON ASSOCIATES	597 FT 182 M	46	2006

156-157 ■ This view from the ground emphasizes the faceted corners formed by the diamond pattern that gives the building its singular appearance.

157 top ■ The Hearst Tower rises above its existing Art Deco style base, whose chamfered corners are decorated with giant columns and statues.

157 bottom ■ The view through the glass roof covering the existing base reveals the structure of the tower and, in the foreground, the huge diagonal supporting elements that characterize the base.

while reflecting much of the solar radiation that generates excessive heat during summer and insulating the interiors from low outside temperatures in winter; and a system of pipes is housed beneath the floor of the large atrium and filled with cooling liquid that absorbs the heat produced.

The tower also has a series of electronic sensors that detect the presence, number and temperature of the people in each area and adjust the operation of the heating, air-conditioning and lighting systems on the basis of this information in order to avoid wasting energy. Even rainwater is collected and used, both to water the gardens in the building and to adjust the level of humidity of the air-conditioning system.

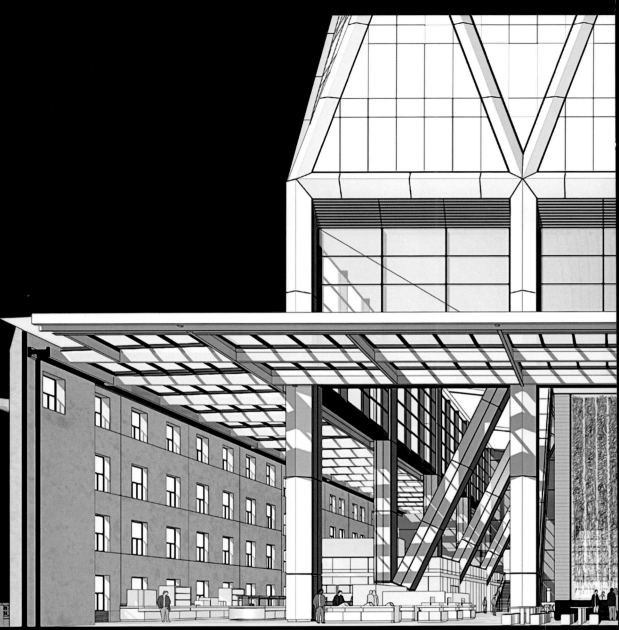

158 bottom ■ The two different levels of
the lobby are connected by three enormous
escalators surrounded by waterfalls.

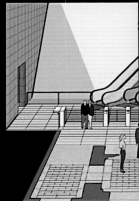

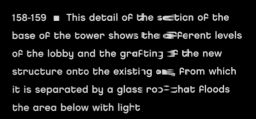

158-159 ■ This detail of the section of the base of the tower shows the different levels of the lobby and the grafting of the new structure onto the existing one, from which it is separated by a glass roof that floods the area below with light.

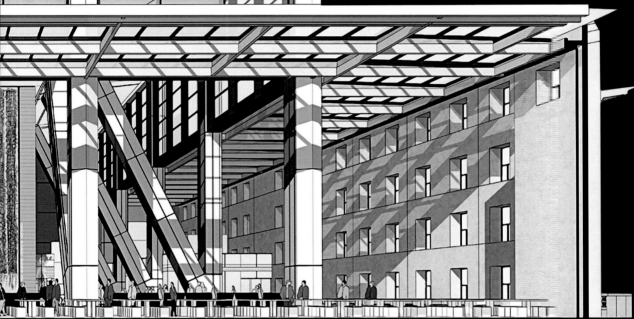

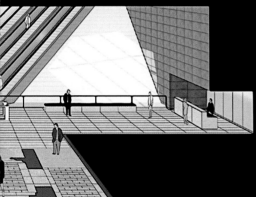

159 bottom ■ The existing base has been completely gutted and is characterized by two levels: a lower one allowing access from the street and an upper one housing a public lobby with cafés, restaurants and meeting places.

ABU DHABI INVESTMENT AUTHORITY TOWER

[ABU DHABI ■ UAE]

The most recent projects by Kohn Pedersen Fox Associates, one of the world's leading designers of skyscrapers, boast sinuous curvy forms that are not simple or assembled cylindrical or elliptical volumes, but figures created by surfaces that bend and curve to envelop the volumes hidden inside them. This trend contrasts with both the forms of the early skyscrapers, which favored geometric solids, and the more recent profusion of other figures derived from the elegant forms of the world of design or nature, such as pinecones, bullets and so on. The figures devised by Kohn Pedersen Fox are also inspired by the natural world, but selected from its most fluid forms, such as sand dunes, wind-filled sails and the spiral as an expression of a dynamic object that evolves and grows. Although proposed as early as 1996 in the firm's three "sails" project in Bangkok, the Daelim Headquarters in Seoul, and the Cooolsingel Project in Rotterdam,

160 ■ The sinuous form of the tower was chosen by Kohn Pedersen Fox Associates to engage with the marine context and the sails in the Gulf, rather than the urban landscape of the area.

161 ■ The façade is composed of a double layer of transparent glass, which gives the tower a uniform appearance while allowing it to function as a bioclimatic building.

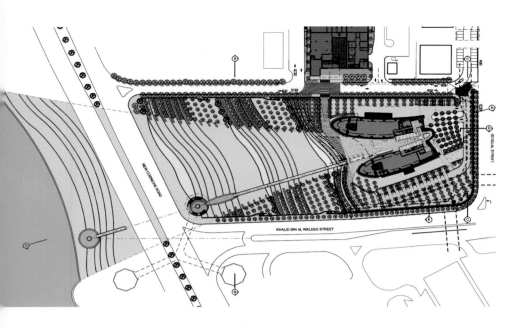

162 top ■ The plan shows
how the façade is folded in
a non-random fashion: the
northern wing is positioned
parallel to the urban grid,
while the southern one is
slightly rotated, allowing
the building to open
towards the sea.

the form was finally built for the first time in the Abu Dhabi Investment
Authority Tower.

162 bottom and 163 ■
The large green area
that extends from the
sea to the tower ends
beneath the imposing
canopy that marks
the building's entrance.

The 38-story ADIA Tower overlooks the sea in a suburban area in which
many international companies have recently started building their headquarters, dominating the skyline of the waterfront with its height and
sinuous silhouette. Its form, which represents a billowing sail, was chosen
to fit in with the seascape, but it also symbolizes the dynamism of Abu
Dhabi as a new international business and financial center.

The height of the curtain wall wrapped around the volume is not constant, but increases to underscore the sense of dynamism and to reveal
its superficial nature, for the actual building is lower than the façade.
The curtain wall is folded in a convex-concave-convex sequence, forming
two wings that house the offices, with a large public atrium between
them. The arrangement of the two wings and the space connecting them
is not random: the highest façade, on the northern side, which then
curves to form the first wing, is positioned parallel to the city grid on
which the rest of the development is built, while the second is slightly rotated, making the building open towards the sea.

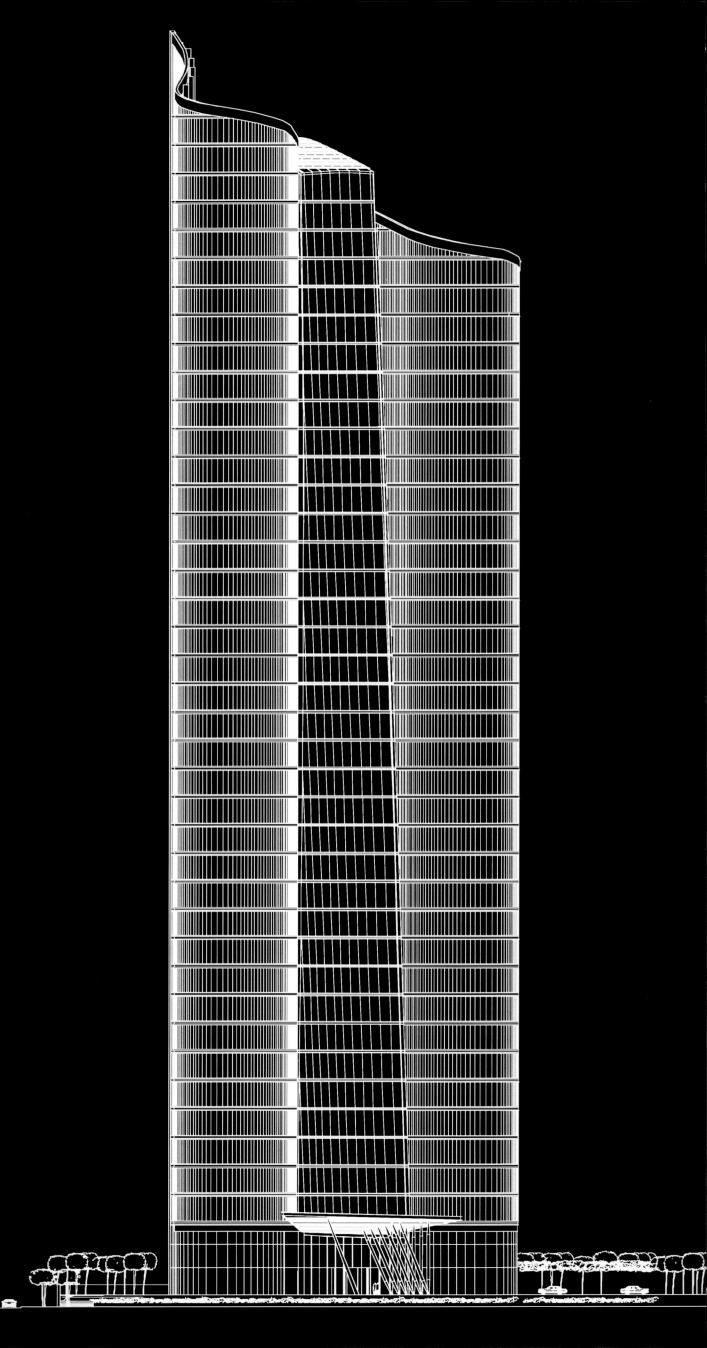

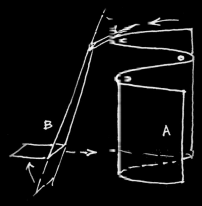

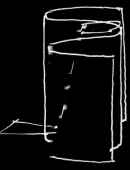

The trapezoid-shaped atrium between the wings is bounded on the east by the circulation shafts. It is crossed by a series of bridges that connect the two wings and stacked gardens at different levels, reinterpreting a typical feature of Islamic architecture in which inside and outside, natural and artificial mingle and merge. This large hollow area also has the function of a solar chimney, in which currents are created that purify the air, while the gardens regulate its humidity and temperature. This is only one of the devices used by KPF to create a building with a low environmental impact, even in an area with such an extreme climate as the Persian Gulf. The tower's skin is composed of a double layer of transparent glass, allowing ventilation and natural lighting, while reducing heat accumulation and consequent energy consumption. The entirely glazed wall and the layout of the offices – both enclosed and open plan – also ensures continuity with the outside space and offers spectacular views.

The continuity of the blue glazed surfaces – with the exception of the west façade, overlaid with a brise-soleil system – gives the building a unitary even appearance, which changes at night when it is illuminated, becoming a sinuous lantern, like a lighthouse on the Abu Dhabi waterfront.

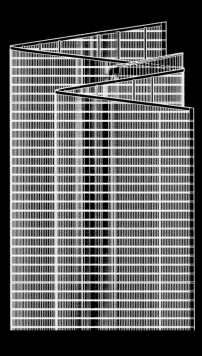

164, 165 center and bottom ■ The various elevations and the section illustrate the arrangement of the tower and the variations produced by the folding of an irregular surface. The sinuous, curvilinear form of the ADIA Tower constitutes an unusual and fanciful addition to the Abu Dhabi skyline, which is very different from the silhouettes of the other buildings in the area.

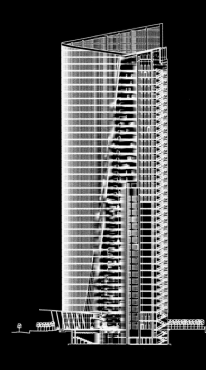

LOCATION	PROJECT	HEIGHT	FLOORS	YEAR
ABU DHABI (UAE)	KOHN PEDERSEN FOX ASSOCIATES	607 FT 185 M	38	2007

166 top ■ The huge open area of the atrium seems to dematerialize at the top of the tower and the façade rises close to the last of the bridges that connect the two wings, creating a sort of panoramic viewpoint from which to admire the views over the Persian Gulf.

166 bottom ■ The base of the tower is entirely glazed and the entrance is situated in the convex part, protected by a large metal canopy supported by enormous rafters.

166-167 ■ The large central atrium is crossed by a series of bridges that connect the two wings and echo the convex shape of the façade.

NEW YORK TIMES TOWER

[NEW YORK ■ USA]

→ →

168 bottom ■ The pure prism of Renzo Piano's tower contrasts with the urban landscape of Times Square, characterized by buildings with bizarre forms, colors and signs.

↑
↑

168-169 ■ The new headquarters of *The New York Times*, on the west side of Times Square has the newspaper's historic masthead screen-printed on the façade, creating a sort of tribute to its setting, where the landscape is defined by advertising signs.

The new headquarters building of *The New York Times*, designed by Renzo Piano, was completed in 2007. The 748-ft (228-m) tower stands on the west side of Times Square on 8th Avenue, between 40th and 41st Street, in one of Manhattan's most central areas. The entire district and the activities based in it are undergoing radical change, due to a huge urban redevelopment plan commenced in the mid-1990s which will progressively replace the quarter's peep shows and strip clubs with cinemas, theaters, hotels and stores. The wide array of cultural diversions is aimed at the new public that has started to settle in the area, changing its social structure. These new buildings use signs and advertising posters to publicize their attractions, creating what some consider an excessively colorful and garish urban landscape that is progressively transforming central Manhattan into a sort of Disneyland. The recent Westin New York at Times Square hotel, designed by Arquitectonica, is emblematic of this trend.

This landscape contrasts strongly with Renzo Piano's design for the New York Times Building that takes the form of a pure prism with a glass façade, offering a simple and elegant image. The Italian architect has tried to convey the vitality of the

170 left ■ This model shows the tower's elegant façade, achieved by the different transparent effects of its various surfaces.

170 right ■ This sketch shows the simple volume proposed by Piano and its skyward continuation in an antenna.

↑
↑

171 ■ The volume of the building is encased in a series of glass surfaces that extend over the entire east and west sides, but cover only the two central modules on the north and south sides.

→→

district and engage with it by creating a series of public areas at the base of the tower instead of using architectural language. Indeed, the building is anchored to the ground by a lobby composed of three transparent volumes accessible from the outside, creating a sequence of spaces continuous with the street. The first is the great atrium running parallel to 8th Avenue, which directs the flows of visitors to the tower's 52 floors that house offices, the headquarters of *The New York Times*, and many other rented premises. Upward access is by means of 28 elevators housed in the central area. The second atrium is home to an internal garden, while the third features three floors of stores, restaurants and meeting places, built above a 378-seat auditorium.

As stressed by Francesco Dal Co in an article published in the Italian magazine *Casabella*, these completely transparent and permeable spaces are profoundly different from the lobbies of traditional skyscrapers, which are prevalently enclosed areas where the entrances mark the passage from the undefined and undistinguished public space of the street to the private sphere that celebrates the power and wealth of the building's owners with exclusive materials, décor and luxury. Instead, Renzo

LOCATION	PROJECT	HEIGHT	FLOORS	YEAR
NEW YORK (USA)	RENZO PIANO BUILDING WORKSHOP, ARCHITECTS, IN COLLABORATION WITH FXFOWLE ARCHITECTS, P.C. (NEW YORK)	1046 FT 319 M	52	2007

Piano has created an area similar to those featured in the type of skyscraper inaugurated by the Citigroup Center in New York, whose open ground floor is public and a continuation of the street.

The base of the New York Times Building is clad in glass panels allowing the visual integration of the interior and the exterior. The same relationship pervades the design of the entire tower: the top is characterized by the extension of the curtain walls above the actual roof (like Piano's Aurora Place in Sydney), in order to make it appear slenderer and create an impression of progressive dematerialization.

Rarefaction, dematerialization and, above all, transparency are the characteristics that the architect has chosen to define the building. In this case, their aesthetic and figurative meaning is also flanked by a symbolic one, for they represent the transparency of the information provided by the newspaper, and the choice to make the building's activities and flows visible relates them to the people in the street, who are the paper's principal readers.

The transparency varies from the base of the tower, defined by a single panel of clear glass, to the top, where the curtain walls are composed of two sheets of glass overlaid with a system of ceramic rods supported by a thin steel frame. The ceramic elements not only create varying degrees of transparency, but also reduce heat absorption and loss ensuring the comfort of the interiors and minimizing energy consumption.

←←

172 ■ **A detail of the diagonal bracing elements that stiffen the structure.**

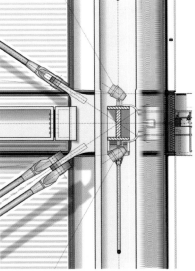

↑
↑

173 top ■ **The curtain walls are composed of two sheets of glass overlaid with a system of ceramic rods supported by a fine steel frame.**

173 bottom ■ **This detail of the structural elements shows the steel beams connected by continuous flanges housing stiffening struts.**

174-175 ■ The transparency of the façade ensures that the tower's interiors are well lit and enjoy spectacular views over Manhattan. The building's base is its most transparent part, allowing the visual integration of the interior and the exterior.

174 bottom ■ This longitudinal section of the building's base shows the sequence of public areas created by the architect: a lobby, a winter garden and a shopping and cultural centre.

175 bottom ■ The workspaces are very open, allowing workers to interact.

←→

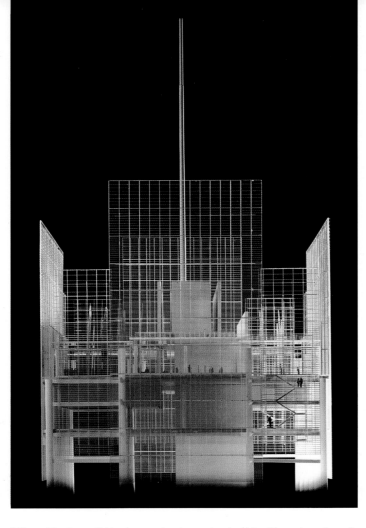

176 ■ The top of the tower is characterized by the extension of the curtain walls above the actual roof, creating an impression of progressive dematerialization as it rises towards the sky.

176-177 ■ The transparency of the façade, particularly when the building is illuminated from inside, makes the newspaper's activities visible and symbolizes the transparency of information.

The light reflected by the rods produces constantly changing color effects, while their spacing becomes gradually closer from the base to the top, forming narrow windows that light the interiors.

The layout of the interiors follows the floor plan, which takes the form of a rectangular grid that coincides with the structural one, featuring 6x5 modules along the perimeter and 4x2 modules in the central core, plus two parts corresponding to the two central modules of the north and south sides, which form a sort of cross.

The building's appearance is derived from the form of the plan and the relationship between façade and structure, for the curtain walls do not form a single volume, but are separate surfaces that extend over the entire fronts on the east and west sides – cladding the structure of steel beams connected by continuous flanges housing stiffening struts – while the curtain wall along 40th and 41st streets covers only the two central modules, leaving the frame exposed on the side ones, which are set back. Here, it also features diagonal bracing in addition to the vertical and horizontal elements. An antenna makes the tower appear even slenderer, allowing it to reach a total height of 1046 ft (319 m). A rooftop garden was originally planned, with fantastic views over the city. However, the space has instead been occupied by plant and water tanks.

Manhattan's regular street plan seems to have been the inspiration for this elegant and extremely slender skyscraper that contrasts with the eccentric buildings that surround it.

CCTV HEADQUARTERS

[BEIJING ■ THE PEOPLE'S REPUBLIC OF CHINA]

The new China Central Television (CCTV) Headquarters is currently being completed in central Beijing, among a series of recently built towers. One of the first of Rem Koolhaas' skyscrapers to be built, it is the concrete result of a series of theories and studies developed by the Dutch architect from 1972, the year in which he visited New York. His visit was followed by a series of writings on skyscrapers, commencing with *Delirious New York: A Retroactive Manifesto for Manhattan* (1978), featuring his Theory of Bigness. More recently, the architect has focused on the development of Asian and particularly Chinese cities in *The Great Leap Forward* (2002). His long career has led him to question the role of the skyscraper and the contemporary relevance of the reasons for which it was developed. He asks himself if its role as symbol of a place and incubator of new ways of life is still pertinent, or if its diffusion has made it so banal that its form is now primarily based on the hopeless race for ultimate height and the activities that it accommodates

178-179 ■ The continuous loop of the CCTV Headquarters and the TVCC with its unbroken pixelated surface stand out from the towers of central Beijing for their innovative and unusual forms.

179 bottom ■ The steel diagrid around the building's perimeter is even more evident in the building under construction.

↑
→

– mainly the offices of multinationals – have become merely routine without producing any new modes of living.

The CCTV Headquarters, however, proposes an unusual form and an innovative function: it is a new type of skyscraper defined by a sculptural form, whose purpose is not to behave as an individual element, detaching itself from its context with a bizarre, alien shape, but as a work of urban architecture that redesigns a piece of city, with which it engages. The two

180 ◼ The two enormous upturned "L"s, connected to form a continuous loop, protect and cover the public space below (the Media Park), forming a large central "window" that frames the surrounding landscape.

LOCATION	PROJECT	HEIGHT	FLOORS	YEAR
BEIJING (THE PEOPLE'S REPUBLIC OF CHINA)	REM KOOLHAAS AND OLE SCHEEREN - OFFICE FOR METROPOLITAN ARCHITECTURE	768 FT 234 M	51	2008

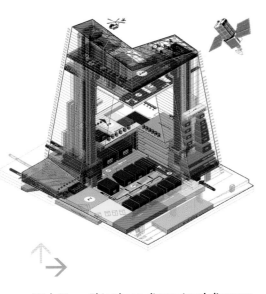

181 left ■ This three-dimensional diagram shows the different activities housed in the building and the base and the way they are connected to each other.

181 right ■ The structural mesh is not regular, but closer in areas subject to greater stress, creating an apparently random pattern. The glass skin, formed of several layers, also follows this irregular design.

enormous upturned "L"s, connected to form a continuous loop that recalls a Möbius strip, envelop and cover the public space below (the Media Park), forming a large central "window" that frames the surrounding landscape and relates to the other tower designed by Koolhaas, the Television Cultural Center (TVCC), which completes the complex with a hotel, a public theater and exhibition facilities. This type of figure, which bends to create a continuous form and a large central cavity that engages and includes the surrounding landscape, recalls the Max Reinhardt Haus in Berlin, designed by Peter Eisenman in 1992, but never built. Although the proportions of Eisenman's building were smaller (34 floors compared to the 55 of the CCTV Headquarters) both structures are sculptural objects on an urban scale, which relate to their settings and create a form that is open to its context and a complex landscape of virtual, natural and artificial features.

This type of architectural form also permits a new way of working, creating a continuous loop of spaces able to house a series of interconnected activities so that the entire television production process can be accommodated in a single building. Indeed the partly underground base is home to recording studios, canteens and gyms, while the two slightly inclined towers that rise from it have different characters: one is dedicated to broadcasting and production facilities, the other to research and information. They merge at the top to create a cantilevered headquarters for management complete with roof garden. These different indoor spaces offer a new type of social life, for their interdependence allows contact and cooperation between the workers of the various sectors. Furthermore, many areas for socialization and meeting, such as canteens and meeting rooms, are located around the ring that connects the working spaces helping to reduce the isolation, rivalry and hierarchies typical of traditional office environments.

The figure of the loop not only characterizes the organizational structure of the network, but also defines the iconic image of Koolhaas' building that transforms the traditional skyscraper – a regular block created from the extrusion of a two-dimensional plan – into a three-dimensional spatial experience, which was made possible by the structural engineering work of Cecil Balmond of Arup. This was no mean feat, for the building was not only required to correspond to the sculptural figure designed by

Koolhaas, but also had to satisfy local planning requirements in a highly seismic zone. The two towers are inclined by 6 degrees with respect to the perpendicular, meaning that each of them acts as a buttress that supports and balances the other (a solution similar to that proposed by Koolhaas for the Hyperbuilding in Bangkok and the Samsung Togok Tower in Seoul, where vertical towers are supported by other smaller ones).

The other structural feature of the CCTV Headquarters is its skin, which takes the form of a diagonal steel grille that encloses the surface of the building and is similar to that used by the Dutch architect for Seattle Central Library. The diagonal steel mesh was originally designed with a regular pattern. However, calculations demonstrating the stress to which the building might be subjected in the case of an earthquake prompted the mesh to be reduced in the most critical areas and widened in those subject to lower stress, creating an irregular and apparently random design, which makes the structure appear even more interesting. The glass envelope behind the mesh also follows this irregular pattern and each pane is cut to measure according to its position in the structural layout. The glass skin is composed of a series of layers that vary according to position, making it transparent in some places and opaque in others. Some areas also house digital screens that transmit images, making the CCTV Headquarters a true media building that produces and broadcasts television programs.

The exterior steel mesh and the two buttresses obviate the need for structural elements inside the building, with the exception of those around the elevators, which were initially designed to be sloping in order to achieve more regular floor plans, but were subsequently positioned vertically to make their construction faster and more straightforward. The arrangement of the building's air-conditioning, heating and ventilation systems also follows the loop that defines its outer image and internal circulation of users.

182-183 ■ In many instances the presence of the diagrid around the perimeter has allowed the interiors to be left free of structural elements.

183 bottom ■ This picture shows the sections of the two towers designed by Koolhaas. That of the CCTV (right) uses different colors to indicate the various activities housed on the different levels. The loop form of the building allows these activities to form a continuous sequence, thus enabling the building to house the entire television production process.

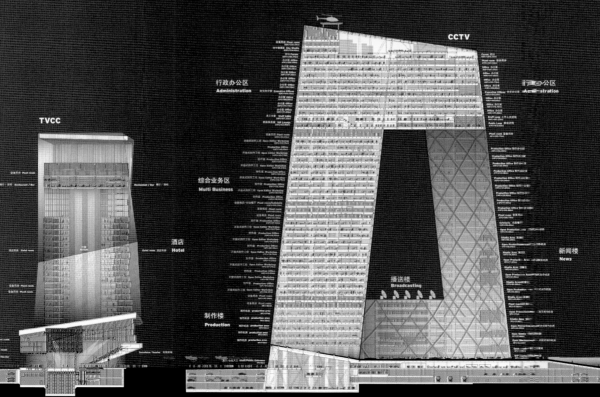

BEIJING YINTAI CENTRE

The Beijing Yintai Centre is a multipurpose complex in the heart of Beijing's business district, near Jianguomenwai Avenue and the World Trade Bridge. The complex was designed by John Portman, an American architect who has always paid great attention to the relationship between buildings and their physical and cultural contexts; he gives much consideration to the spaces and the people who inhabit them in an environment combining natural and artificial elements. His project for the Beijing Yintai Centre draws on the same theme, using a simple functional form that engages with its setting by means of motifs drawn from the local culture.

The complex is formed by three towers: twin office blocks, 610 ft (186 m) high with 45 stories, which stand either side of a 820-ft (250-m) building housing a hotel. All three towers have a square plan and a regular form, echoed in the square steel and aluminum grid that characterizes the curtain-wall façades of their exterior. This insistent regularity is broken only by the crown of the central tower, which takes the form of a cube, slightly detached from the rest of the building, and features a different pattern recalling a Chinese lantern, associating the structure with the local culture. During the day it marks the Beijing Yintai Centre on the city's skyline, while at night, it is illuminated and shines like a lantern over the Chinese capital.

A podium connects the bases of the three towers. Inside Portman has created a multistoried atrium – a feature also present in his American buildings – whose levels overlook each other and offer visitors lobbies, meeting places, stores and restaurants. Major roads with heavy traffic surround the area in

184-185 ■ The three towers are connected at the base and take the form of regular rectangular blocks, whose distinctive feature is constituted by the square pattern of the steel and aluminum curtain walls.

→→

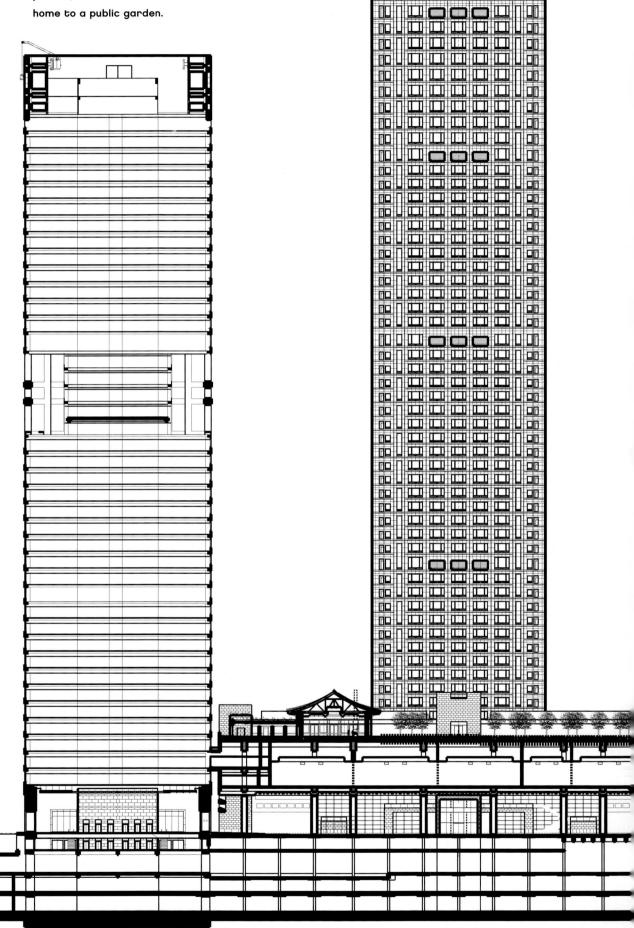

186-187 ■ The longitudinal
section reveals the
regularity of the twin
towers destined for
offices, with the exception
of the large entrance
lobbies and the central
podium, whose roof is
home to a public garden.

LOCATION	PROJECT	HEIGHT	FLOORS	YEAR
BEIJING (THE PEOPLE'S REPUBLIC OF CHINA)	JOHN PORTMAN & ASSOCIATES	CENTRAL 820 FT 250 M - SIDE 610 FT 186 M	CENTRAL 63 SIDE 43	2008

187 ■ Each tower has an
entrance lobby arranged
on several levels, which
overlook each other and
offer visitors meeting
places, stores and
restaurants.

which the complex is located. Consequently, Portman has featured a grand entrance to each tower beneath the podium, allowing motor access to the complex.

The Beijing Yintai Centre aims to create a setting in which residents may retreat from the outside world, with its congested streets, heavy traffic and pollution, to a natural landscape or several interconnected levels. The project features plants and water, which also characterize the great entrance halls of Portman's American hotels. Indeed, the roof of the podium has landscaped gardens that reach down to street to create a multi-level urban park. Plants and water are used to create an area removed from the surrounding congested streets, creating a traditional Chinese space – the small garden – by incorporating natural features in the architecture.

Each tower has been designed and planned to perform a specific function: the tallest core is defined by a central core containing the circulation shafts that allow access to the 237 rooms and the 180 luxury apartments, while the core of the twin towers is divided into four allowing each of them to function as four separate buildings, each with its own entrance hall and a sky-lobby on the roof.

SHANGHAI WORLD FINANCIAL CENTER

[SHANGHAI ■ THE PEOPLE'S REPUBLIC OF CHINA]

When it was commissioned from Kohn Pedersen Fox in 1994, the Shanghai World Financial Center was intended to become the tallest building in the world, symbolizing China's economic development, and one of the greatest icons of the Asian landscape. However, a series of problems led to the interruption of work and the partial redesign of the structure. While the SWFC may not be the world's tallest building, it is nonetheless the highest landmark in China. It is situated in the Lujiazui district of the Pudong area of Shanghai, which has recently witnessed the construction of a series of skyscrapers, with the most diverse forms. These structures house the headquarters of leading Chinese multinationals, luxury hotels and residential units, such as the Jin Mao Building – the technological pagoda built by Skidmore, Owings & Merrill in 1998.

The elegant linear Shanghai World Financial Center stands in the heart of this district and contrasts with the complex silhouettes of the other towers, for it is one of those skyscrapers that seems to be inspired by the world of design objects rather than local or global building traditions. It can be likened to design objects in its quest for elegant, apparently elementary forms that are actually complex plastic shapes, allowing it to be de-

189 top ◼ The picture shows
the tower during construction.
Its monolithic shape, derived from the
world of design, contrasts with that
of the nearby Jin Mao Building, which
evokes the image of a pagoda, a form
drawn from the local tradition.

188-189 ◼ The elegant linear Shanghai
World Financial Center stands out on
the complex Shanghai skyline.

189 bottom ◼ The glass and steel façade
emphasizes the building's smooth abstract
form, differentiating it from the
surrounding towers, which are marked
by the pattern of their floors.

fined as a "singular object," for it is devoid of the typical features of a building, such as
windows, belt courses and so on. The distinctive characteristic of such structures is
their original, bizarre and even "monstrous" form, and they stand alone within the global landscapes.

The form of the Shanghai World Financial Center was created by merging a square
prism – a traditional Chinese symbol of the Earth – with two arches, which causes it to
taper progressively upward until becoming a single line at the top, corresponding to the
diagonal of the square base. Its apparent simplicity actually conceals a highly complex
plan generated by its progressive narrowing, which means that each floor is different,
allowing the various functions housed in the building to be accommodated in the most
suitable area. Indeed, the building has offices and conference rooms on the lower floors,
a luxurious 300-room hotel on the higher ones, and restaurants and an observatory
around the large aperture in the top of the tower. This distinctive feature was originally
conceived as a circular opening to symbolize the Chinese moon gate (an entrance in a garden wall shaped like a full moon). However, it was considered too similar to the rising sun

190 left ■ The section shows the arrangement of the building's different functions: the base houses a shopping mall, the lower part of the tower the offices, the upper floors a hotel, and the summit a panoramic viewpoint and restaurants.

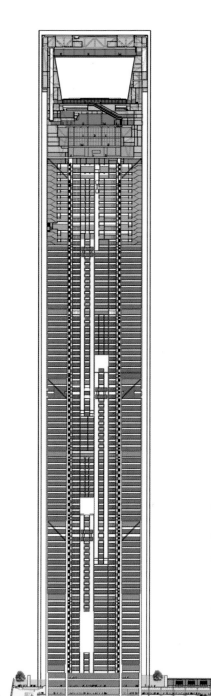

of the Japanese flag and was thus replaced with a trapezoidal opening that, while making the tower appear more banal and less streamlined, had the advantage of being accepted by the city's inhabitants, as well as being easier and less costly to build. The opening also has the important function of reducing wind pressure, allowing the tower to reach a height of 1614 ft (492 m).

The Shanghai World Financial Center's elegant streamlined silhouette and glass and steel cladding that emphasizes its monolithic simplicity make it a "singular object," without the usual functional or decorative architectural elements. The base of the tower is a stone-clad podium. This material and the areas that it houses allow it to engage with people on a human scale, unlike the tower itself. It is home to a shopping mall and a grand entrance hall that directs the flows of visitors toward the various activities housed on the upper floors.

190 right and 191 ■ The two profiles of the tower illustrate the origins of its volume, created from the intersection of a square prism with two arcs that converge in the diagonal of the square base at its summit.

LOCATION	PROJECT	HEIGHT	FLOORS	YEAR
SHANGHAI (THE PEOPLE'S REPUBLIC OF CHINA)	KOHN PEDERSEN FOX ASSOCIATES	1614 FT 492 M	101	2008

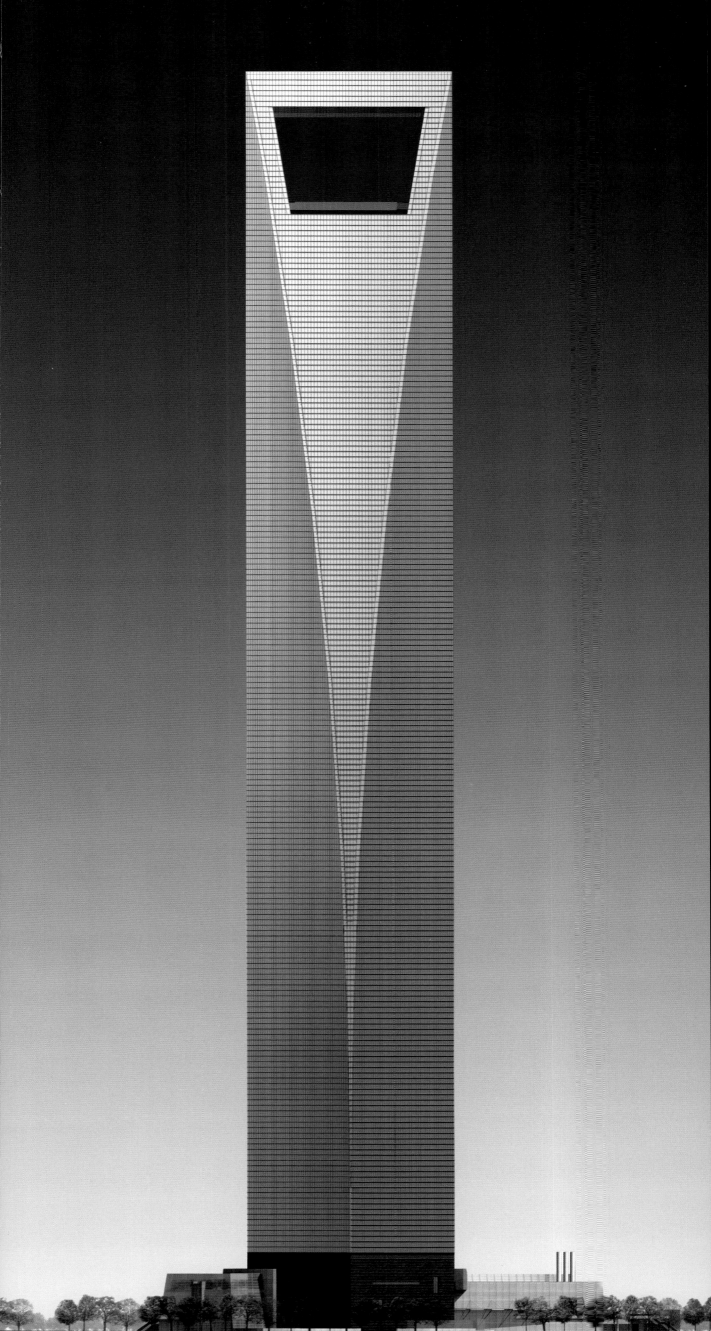

BURJ DUBAI

[DUBAI ▪ UAE]

The United Arab Emirates are fast becoming the site of a concentration of many impressive works designed by leading international architects. These projects set out to outdo the Western World by constructing the tallest building in the world (which in fact had already occurred with the construction of the Petronas Towers at Kuala Lumpur), and the most ecological and technologically advanced one, and also to vie with the West on another level through the construction of prestigious cultural complexes. While the true objective of these projects is to promote and develop tourism in the region, they have also become a sort of local competition in which each nation is trying to go one better than its neighbors. This is especially true of Abu Dhabi and Dubai, which seem to be the main competitors. For example, on the island of Saadiyat at Abu Dhabi work is underway on a cultural center that includes a branch of the Guggenheim Museum designed by Frank Gehry, a branch of the Louvre by Jean Nouvel, the Maritime Museum by Tadao Ando, and a complex of opera houses designed by Zaha Hadid. In the meantime, Norman Foster is designing Masdar, a city that will be free of both pollution and garbage. At Dubai, after the Burj al Arab, the tallest hotel in the world, and the Dubai Mall, the largest shopping mall on our planet, the construction of the Burj Dubai, which will be the world's tallest building, is underway. Its actual height is being kept secret so that it cannot be surpassed during construction work, but there is talk of more than 160 stories and about 2684 ft (about 818 m). The project was awarded to SOM (Skidmore, Owings & Merrill LLP), one of the world's most famous firms in the field of skyscraper construction, which boasts such celebrated creations as the Sears Tower in Chicago, the Freedom Tower in New York, and the future Infinity Tower in Dubai. In 2003 SOM won the competition promoted by Emaar Properties PJSC for a complex that will include offices, a five-star hotel, 700 private apartments, shopping centers, a swimming pool and, on the 123rd and 124th floors, a panoramic terrace connected to the rest of the complex by means of the fastest elevator in the world, which will move at a speed of 59 ft (18 m) per second. The Burj Dubai lies in a central area featuring

192-193 ▪ Although situated in an area with many recently built skyscrapers, Burj Dubai's gargantuan dimensions mean that the tower dwarfs the surrounding buildings, appearing out of context in downtown Dubai.

193 bottom ▪ This view of the tower from the ground emphasizes its form, which rises from a massive base and gradually tapers to the tip of the antenna, 2684 feet (818 m) above the ground, by means of a series of setbacks.

← →

194 top ■ This plan shows the area in which Burj Dubai is located, on a small manmade island in the center of an artificial lake, surrounded by a series of lower towers.

195 ■ The form of the tower, shown full height here, is based on an abstracted version of the desert flower *Hymenocallis*, and follows an upward spiraling pattern, in which its cross section decreases as it reaches toward the sky.

many other recently built skyscrapers, including the Emirates Twin Towers. Like the other buildings in the city, these latter reach a height of 1165 ft (355 m), but do not constitute a true skyline together with the new SOM tower, which will be so high that it has been conceived as an isolated object that will be seen from a distance of 60 miles (90 km). Its shape is modeled after that of a desert flower, the *Hymenocallis*, which is extremely popular in Dubai. As is the case with Oriental skyscrapers, this type of architecture combines an element of local culture – the bamboo used for Tapei 101, the pagoda in the Petronas Towers complex – with the technical and engineering features necessary for a building of this size. In fact, the tower, much like the desert flower, has a spiral shape that soars toward the sky while gradually tapering. As a result, the base is particularly broad and the top will be slender. The plan of the tower calls for three elements, three linked petals around a central nucleus made of reinforced concrete and containing the vertical distribution elements. Each petal has its own structural nucleus and a series of reinforced concrete columns on the perimeter and is rotated and set back with respect to the one before it in order to give the impression of growth while at the same time progressively reducing the weight of the tower. Only the central nucleus, made of steel, will remain on the top, crowned by an antenna that will make for a total height of about 2684 ft (818 m). The progressively diminishing stages – an archetypal figure of the American skyscraper connected with building regulations but also of the history of architecture, for example, with the ziggurat – allows us to place the Burj Dubai in a foreseeable future rather than in the category of science fiction. Furthermore, the glass exterior means that the interior will have natural illumination, while the "Y" shape of the plan optimizes the possibility to vary the views of the Persian Gulf.

↑
↑

194 bottom ■ This plan of Dubai shows how the area is characterized by a series of features – artificial islands and lakes, dizzily tall towers, etc. – in which the power of technology has conquered the natural landscape, which has been completely manipulated by man.

LOCATION	PROJECT	HEIGHT	FLOORS	YEAR
DUBAI (UAE)	SKIDMORE, OWINGS & MERRILL LLP	2684 FT 818 M	162	2009

BURJ QATAR

196 ■ **The Burj Qatar is surrounded by greenery. The plan of the tower emphasizes its circular form, its structure with pairs of columns around the edge and its asymmetrically positioned structural core.**

Competition between the various Gulf States and the wish to acquire prestige has led to a myriad of projects in the region by the most renowned international architects, including Jean Nouvel, who has designed both the Louvre Museum in Abu Dhabi and an office tower in Doha, Qatar. Both are part of a much larger cultural program that the various Gulf States are implementing, as though the record of the world's highest building, about to be completed in Dubai, had been joined by a new reason for competing; namely the construction of a huge cultural center capable of shifting the current emphasis away from the West. Consequently, the project for an office tower was not assigned to one of the various architectural firms specializing in high-rise buildings, but to an internationally renowned architect, capable of proposing an iconic and extremely elegant figure that engages with its setting.

Jean Nouvel's new building is part of a larger scheme commissioned by the National Council of Culture, Arts and Heritage, which features the construction of a series of buildings and the remodeling of the Corniche, which will give the shoreline of the Bay of Doha a facelift. The French architect's tower, due to be inaugurated in 2010, is situated between the Corniche and the city center and marks the landscape with a geyser-like form that rises above the water, echoing that of the Torre Agbar in Barcelona. Indeed, it shares the same circular plan, which is a sort of constant in Nouvel's towers (it was also featured in the Tour Sans Fins designed for Paris' La Défense district) with an asymmetrically positioned structural core housing the circulation shafts. However, in the Doha tower, this is constituted by a series of offset parallelepipeds instead of a cylinder, as in its Barcelona counterpart.

The tower's cylindrical plan and the central core allow the workspaces to be positioned around the circular perimeter of the façade, maximizing the natural light and allowing them to enjoy spectacular views, in this case of the Persian Gulf to the east, the port to the south, the city to the east, and the coast and desert to the north. The Burj

197 ■ **The design of the skin was inspired by the motifs of the Islamic _moucharaby_. The effects that it creates vary according to the intensity of the light.**

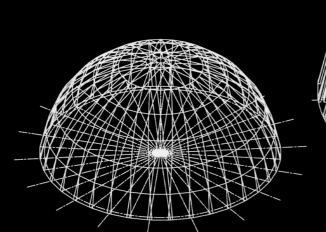

198 ▼ These axonometric projections illustrate the details of the steel structure of the tower's dome: top left, the arrangement of the structural elements; bottom left, the diagrid that supports the glass panels; right, the two superimposed structures.

Qatar differs from the Torre Agbar in its structure and skin, as well as an antenna that allows it to reach a height of 760 ft (231 m).

In Doha, the concrete structural skin of the Barcelona tower has been replaced by a series of angled steel and concrete elements that form a diagrid encasing its curved form, using the same technique adopted by Norman Foster for 30 St Mary Axe in London and the Hearst Tower in New York. However, in the Burj Qatar it is not visible from the outside, for it is covered by a stratified skin that constitutes the most distinctive element of the structure, defining the image of the tower and its relationship to its setting. It is created by the use of a highly technological device, similar to that used by Nouvel in 1987 for the Arab World Institute in Paris, which evokes an architectural feature deeply rooted in Islamic culture: the *moucharaby*. The intricate decorative motifs have been removed from their original handcrafted context and transformed into the innovative and extremely technological skin of the tower. The latticework assumes different thicknesses according to its position and thus exposure to the sun: 80 percent to the east and west, 40 percent to the south, and 25 percent to the north. It is formed by four butterfly-shaped aluminum elements of four different sizes, allowing the openness of the mesh to vary. As in the Arab World Institute building, this device interacts with the light, characterizing the interiors and protecting them

LOCATION	PROJECT	HEIGHT	FLOORS	YEAR
DOHA (QATAR)	ATELIERS JEAN NOUVEL	760 FT 231 M	44	2010

199 right ■ Lit from inside, the Burj Qatar reveals all the layers that compose the tower: the inner structural diagrid, the glass façade and the protective sunshade system.

→ →

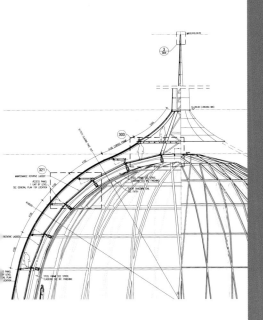

199 left ■ A detail of the section of the dome showing the aluminum elements on the outside, the glass panels with their structure in the middle, and the steel structure of the dome on the inside.

↑
↑

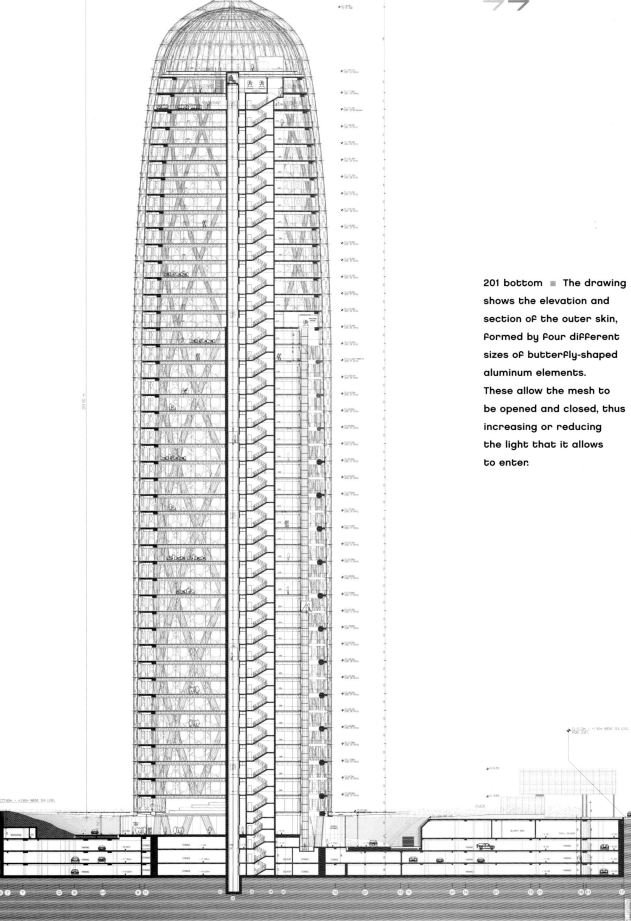

201 top ■ This axonometric
projection and detail show
the superimposition and
connection of the various
aluminum elements that
form the sunshade system.

201 bottom ■ The drawing
shows the elevation and
section of the outer skin,
formed by four different
sizes of butterfly-shaped
aluminum elements.
These allow the mesh to
be opened and closed, thus
increasing or reducing
the light that it allows
to enter.

200 ■ This north-south section of the building shows the entrance at the base of the tower,
protected by a glass canopy and accessed via a sloping garden; the asymmetric position of
the core housing the circulation shafts; and the domed top.

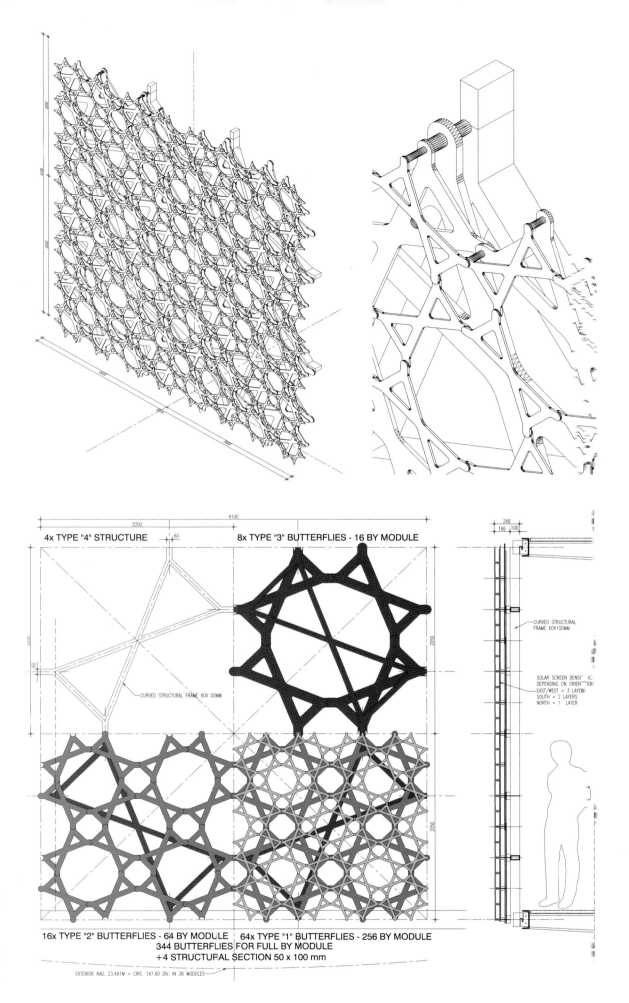

4x TYPE "4" STRUCTURE

8x TYPE "3" BUTTERFLIES - 16 BY MODULE

CURVED STRUCTURAL FRAME 60X 00MM

CURVED STRUCTURAL
FRAME 60X100MM

SOLAR SCREEN DENSIT V::
DEPENDING ON ORIEN 10::
EAST/WEST = 3 LAYE::
SOUTH = 2 LAYERS
NORTH = 1 LAYER

16x TYPE "2" BUTTERFLIES - 64 BY MODULE   64x TYPE "1" BUTTERFLIES - 256 BY MODULE
344 BUTTERFLIES FOR FULL BY MODULE
+4 STRUCTURAL SECTION 50 x 100 mm

EXTERIOR RAD. 23.491M = CIRC. 147.60 DIV. IN 36 MODULES

from solar radiation by a succession of layers: an outermost aluminum one, an inner one of re-fractive glass, and an additional one – given that the building is situated in the Persian Gulf – composed of shutters able to screen out even more sunlight.

At the base of the tower lies a sloping garden that leads down to the entrance, situated below street level and marked by a huge glass canopy, which allows access to an enormous atrium 367 ft (112 m) high. It is amazing how Jean Nouvel always manages to create extremely innovative designs using the same techniques and materials, and thus continue his quest into the possible relationships between materials and light, which allows him to create unexpected effects each time.

LEADENHALL BUILDING

[LONDON ■ UK]

The Leadenhall Building by Richard Rogers occupies a strategic site in the City of London (London's financial center) between the Aviva Tower, built in International Style in 1969 (the first building to have exceeded the height of St Paul's Cathedral), the recent 30 St Mary Axe (or Swiss Re Tower) by Norman Foster, and the Pinnacle by Kohn Pedersen Fox, still at the planning stage.

This group of skyscrapers will profoundly change the London skyline with a series of original and bizarre silhouettes, ranging from Foster's pinecone to Kohn Pedersen Fox's spiral and the wedge shape of the Leadenhall Building that, at 737 ft (225 m) in height, is second only to the Pinnacle, which will rise 945 ft (288 m). Nearby is the site of Renzo Piano's planned pyramidal London Bridge Tower and the existing hexagonal Tower 42.

Rogers' design was not only influenced by his wish to distinguish the building from its neighbors, but also by the need to avoid obstructing the sightlines, and particularly the view of St Paul's Cathedral from Fleet Street. Although not actually protected by law, these viewing corridors are strenuously defended by English Heritage, which intervenes each time they are threatened.

The Leadenhall tower is composed of two distinct parts: a gradually tapering shape that houses offices and a lower regular rectangular support core with elevators, part

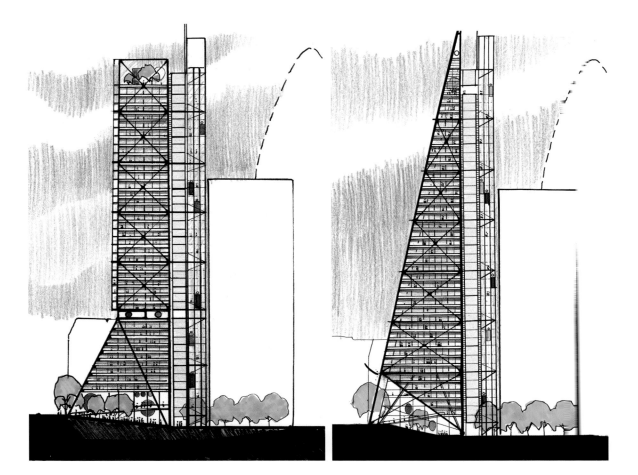

202 ■ The Leadenhall Building's sloping façade gives the tower an original slender form that engages with the dynamism of the Lloyd's building that stands opposite it.

203 ■ The wedge-shaped design has considerable advantages, as it does not obstruct the view of St Paul's, while allowing more spacious floors for the offices and better natural lighting of the interiors.

204 bottom ■ The distinctive wedge shape of the Leadenhall Building was designed to avoid obstructing the sightlines of St Paul's Cathedral.

machinery and plumbing, which is separate from the former but connected to it. This structural core is situated on the northern side of the building, avoiding the need to cover the steel frame with fireproof materials and thus altering its appearance.

Both parts are clad with glass, revealing both the steel frame and the people moving around inside the building. The appearance of the supporting structure is made more dynamic by three groups of elevators and by the use of color.

204-205 ■ Richard Rogers'
Leadenhall Building and Norman
Foster's 30 St Mary Axe
transform the London skyline with
their bizarre figures that offer a
strong contrast to the traditional
skyscrapers of the City

205 bottom ■ The diagrams
show the different sections
studied by Roger before finding
the definitive solution. All feature
two distinct volumes: one
containing the service areas
and the other housing the offices.

LOCATION	PROJECT	HEIGHT	FLOORS	YEAR
LONDON (UK)	RICHARD ROGERS PARTNERSHIP	737 FT 225 M	50	2011

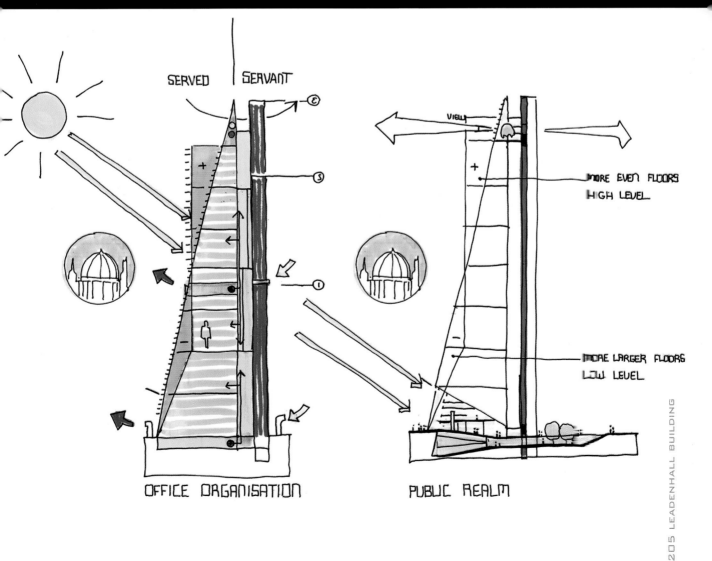

OFFICE ORGANISATION

PUBLIC REALM

The part of the building housing the offices has a double layer of glass enclosing ventilation ducts that regulate the flow of air, while ensuring natural lighting and preventing reflection and heat loss. A third inner layer allows the interiors to be shaded in the case of excessive sunlight.

It was feared that the high density of the new tower blocks under construction could result in the loss of the public space that has always characterized this area. In order to avoid this danger Rogers has designed the building to leave an open space that connects St Helen's Square with Leadenhall Street. This is achieved via a sloping platform and the space forms a public plaza with gardens at the base of the tower, completely surrounded by glass walls, creating the illusion of another outdoor space. It can be accessed from various directions in order to maintain the area's traditional pedestrian links. This large public atrium, 100 ft (30.5 m) high, is crossed by three large escalators allowing access to the various levels that overlook it. These levels have restaurants, cafés and terraces.

Continuity between inside and outside space is further emphasized by the sloping façade, which is bent to form a canopy marking the entrance to the tower.

←←

206 ■ The tower's northern façade is characterized by the regular volume that houses the circulation shafts. Its glass walls allow the movements inside it to be seen from the street, creating a dynamic effect.

207 top ■ The base of the tower features a large public lobby that can be accessed from different directions, forming a continuous urban space with the street.

207 bottom ■ The lobby is a 98-ft (30 m) high glazed space housing gardens and benches, creating the sensation of an outdoor area.

THE PINNACLE

[LONDON ■ UK]

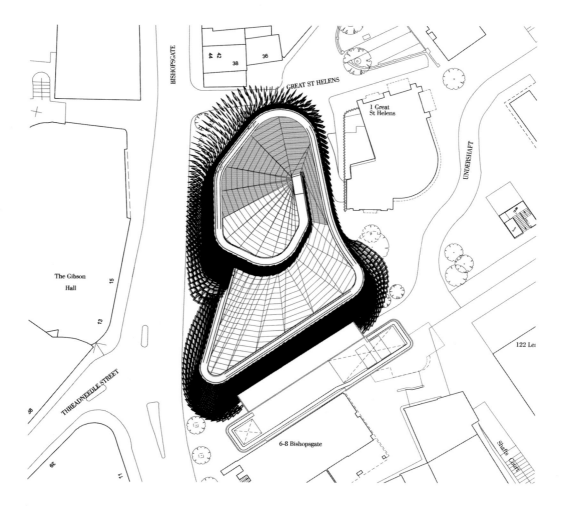

The largest and tallest tower on the City of London skyline will be the Pinnacle, previously known as the Bishopsgate Tower, designed by Kohn Pedersen Fox. It is one of a series of new landmarks that is radically changing the appearance of the heart of the British capital. London seems destined to become Europe's leading economic and financial center and needs new icons to represent its newly acquired power in the public imagination.

Several international firms, including the German fund management company DIFA, have managed to purchase areas or existing buildings in the heart of the City to construct their headquarters and have commissioned the world's leading architects to design them. While London is a European capital that has long been home to innovative structures, such as Richard Rogers' Lloyd's building, these have always had to comply with the constraints imposed by the Civic Aviation Guidelines and English Heritage, which prevents interference with the sightlines of St Paul's Cathedral. These limitations also posed a problem for architects Murphy/Jahn from whom the Bishopsgate Tower project was initially commissioned, as English Heritage strongly opposed their proposal of a 708-ft (216-m) cylindrical tower wrapped in a transparent skin. The commission was consequently assigned to Kohn Pedersen Fox and moved

208 ■ The plan of the tower's roof illustrates its form, created by a surface wrapped around itself, with the highest point in the center.

209 ■ The City of London skyline will soon be transformed by a series of towers with bizarre forms designed by the world's leading architects.

210-211 ■ **The Pinnacle's glazed surface wraps around itself to form a spiral that defines the tower's image from the top to the base, where the glass skin flares out to form a canopy protecting the public area in front of the entrance.**

From 6-8 Bishopsgate to the adjoining area of Crosby Court, in order avoid obstructing the view of St Paul's Cathedral.

The tower was initially designed to be 1007 ft (307 m) high, but Britain's Civil Aviation Authority insisted that its height be reduced to 945 ft (288 m). Its spiral form is more dynamic and plastic than that proposed by Murphy/Jahn because the building is created by the movement of a surface wrapped around itself. The Pinnacle is thus defined by its surface rather than volumetric configuration, which creates a slender, light, dynamic building. Indeed, it is one of the most successful examples of this type of structure, which is widely featured in the recent production of the American architectural firm, from the Parkhaven Tower in Rotterdam to the ADIA headquarters in Abu Dhabi.

The success of such buildings lies in their cladding, which in all these cases is constituted by a transparent skin. In the London building this works like a snakeskin, composed of a series of overlapping panels that follow the curved form of the structure and ensure transparency and continuity, as they hide the frame.

All the panels are the same size, in order to reduce production costs, and form a ventilated wall inside which air can circulate. The glass skin flares out from the tower toward its base to form a sort of skirt that emphasizes and protects the public area below.

Indeed, the building's location between Bishopsgate and Crosby Square means that its base is divided in two by a public footpath that connects them and allows pedestrians to traverse the area. This path is lined with a series of public areas, while others are situated on the 43rd floor, which houses a sky-lobby and a restaurant with panoramic views over the City. The base of the tower also offers three levels of stores on the basement floors, as well as stores and restaurants on the first three stories. The rest of the tower houses 950,000 sq. ft (88,258 sq. m) of office space on 56 floors.

The Pinnacle, like other buildings designed by Kohn Pedersen Fox, is equipped with energy-saving features, such as the solar panels at the top of the spiral that allow the building to be partially self-sufficient in terms of energy production.

LOCATION	PROJECT	HEIGHT	FLOORS	YEAR
LONDON (UK)	KOHN PEDERSEN FOX ASSOCIATES	945 FT 288 M	63	2011

bibliography

Matteo Agnoletto, *Groundzero.exe. Costruire il vuoto*, Kappa Edizioni, Bologna 2004.

Jean Baudrillard, *Jean Nouvel, Les objets singuliers. Architecture et philosophie*, Essais-Calmann-Lévy, Editions de la Villette, Paris 2000.

Mario Campi, *Skyscrapers. An architectural Type of Modern Urbanism*, ETH Zurich Department of Architecture, Birkhauser, Basel 2000.

Warren I. Cohen and Olivo Barbieri, *Il secolo del Pacifico. Asia e America al centro del mondo-Notsofareast. Immagini tra Pechino e Shanghai*, Donzelli, Rome 2002.

Nik Cohn, *The Heart of the World*, Knopf, New York 1992.

Michela Comba, Carlo Olmo and Manfredo di Robilant ed., *Un grattacielo per la spina. Torino 6 progetti su una centralità urbana*, Allemandi, Turin 2007.

Don DeLillo, *Falling Man*, Scribner, New York 2008.

Judith Dupré, *Gratte-ciel du monde - Une histoire des plus célèbres gratte-ciel du monde*, Könemann, Köln 1996.

Eric J. Hobsbawm, *Age of Extremes - The Short Twentieth Century 1914-1991*, Pantheon Books - Random House, New York 1994.

Eric Höweler, *Skyscraper: Vertical Now*, Universe Publishing, New York 2003.

Thomas Kelly, *Empire Rising: A Novel*, Picador USA, New York 2006.

Rem Koolhaas, *Delirious New York: a Retroactive Manifesto for Manhattan*, Oxford University Press, New York 1978.

Rem Koolhaas, *Content*, Taschen, Köln 2003.

Rowan Moore, *Vertigo: The Strange New World of the Contemporary City*, Laurence King Publishing, London 1999.

Next 8. Mostra Internazionale di Architettura, la Biennale di Venezia, catalogo, Edizioni Marsilio, Padua 2002.

Antonino Terranova, *Mostri Metropolitani*, Meltemi Editore, Roma 2001.

Antonino Terranova, *Scolpire i cieli. Scritti sui grattacieli moderni e contemporanei* (a cura di Luca Massidda), Officina Edizioni, Roma 2006.

index

index

index

photo credits

photo credits

Page 157 bottom Chuck Choi/Arcaid/Corbis

Page 158 Orjan F. Ellingvag/ Dagens Naringsliv/Corbis

Pages 158-159 Courtesy of Foster + Partners

Page 159 Chuck Choi/Arcaid/Corbis

Pages 160, 161, 162 bottom, 163 H.G. Esch

Pages 162 top, 164, 165 Courtesy of Kohn Pedersen Fox Associates

Pages 166 top, 166 bottom, 167 H.G. Esch

Page 168 Courtesy of Renzo Piano Building Workshop

Pages 168-169 Renzo Piano/Michel Denancé/Artedia

Page 170 left Michel Denancé/Piano Renzo/ Artedia

Page 170 right Courtesy of Renzo Piano Building Workshop

Page 171 Serge Drouin

Page 172 Michel Denancé/Piano Renzo/ Artedia

Page 173 top Michel Denancé/Piano Renzo/ Artedia

Pages 173 bottom, 174 Courtesy of Renzo Piano Building Workshop

Pages 174-175, 175, 176 Renzo Piano/Michel Denancé/Artedia

Page 177 Michel Denancé/Piano Renzo/Artedia

Pages 178-179 Courtesy of Office for Metropolitan Architecture

Page 179 Tom van Dillen

Page 180, 181 left and right, 182-183, 183 Courtesy of Office for Metropolitan Architecture

Pages 184-185, 186-187, 187 Courtesy of John Portman & Associates, Inc

Pages 188-189 Superview, courtesy of Kohn Pedersen Fox Associates

Page 189 top ChinaFotoPress

Page 189 bottom Philip Gostelow/Anzenberger/ Contrasto

Page 190 top Superview, courtesy of Kohn Pedersen Fox Associates

Page 190 bottom Courtesy of Kohn Pedersen Fox Associates

Page 191 Superview, courtesy of Kohn Pedersen Fox Associates

Pages 192-193 Chris Jackson/Getty Images

Page 193 Courtesy of Andisart

Page 194 top Courtesy of BurjDubaiSkyscrapers

Page 194 bottom Courtesy of Nakheel

Page 195 Business Wire/Getty Images

Page 196 top and bottom, 197, 198, 199 left and right, 200, 201 top and bottom Courtesy of Ateliers Jean Nouvel

Page 202 Cityscape, courtesy of Rogers Stirk Harbour + Partners

Pages 203, 204, 205 Courtesy of Rogers Stirk Harbour + Partners

Page 204-205 Eamonn O'Mahony, courtesy of Rogers Stirk Harbour + Partners

Pages 206, 207 top and bottom Cityscape, courtesy of Rogers Stirk Harbour + Partners

Page 208 Courtesy of Kohn Pedersen Fox Associates

Pages 209 and 211 Cityscape, courtesy of Kohn Pedersen Fox Associates

acknowledgments

The Publisher would like to thank:

Arata Isozaki & Associates, Tokyo, Takako Fujimoto

Arquitectonica, Miami, Dennis Wilhelm

Ateliers Jean Nouvel, Paris, Charlotte Huisman

Santiago Calatrava, New York, Claire Whittaker

Foster + Partners, London, Kathryn Tollervey

Massimiliano Fuksas Architect, Rome, Lucia Bosso

HOK - Hellmuth, Obata & Kassabaum, St Louis, Mike Plotnick

Invicta Public Affairs, Edinburgh, Laura Maddison

Kohn Pedersen Fox Associates, London, Elizabeth Walker

Costas Kondylis and Partners LLP, Architects, New York, Vincent Hokia and Gregory Saliola

Dennis Lau & Ng Chun Man Architects & Engineers (HK) Ltd, Hong Kong, Liby Kwok

C.Y. Lee & Partners, Taipei, Zoe Lin

Studio Daniel Libeskind, New York, Lynn Krogh

Llewelyn Davies Yeang, London, Ken Yeang

Mecanoo Architecten b.v., Delft, Machteld Schoep

mOrphosis, Santa Monica, Anne Marie Burke and Lauren Rosenbloom

Murphy/Jahn, Chicago, Keith H. Palmer and Jason E. Brooks

Nakheel, Dubai, Aaron Richardson and Shabana Sonde

Office for Metropolitan Architecture [OMA], Rotterdam, Isabel Pagel

Peichl & Partner ZT GmbH, Wien, Ursula Brandl-Straka

Pelli Clarke Pelli Architects, New Haven, Diana Daly

Renzo Piano Building Workshop, Genoa, Chiara Casazza, Giovanna Giusto and Stefania Canta

John Portman & Associates, Atlanta, Luca Maffey and Emily Ann Munnell

RMJM, London, Andrea Braga and Nicola Martin

Rocco Design Architects Ltd., Hong Kong, Freddie Hai

Rogers Stirk Harbour + Partners, London, Jenny Stephens

Skidmore, Owings & Merrill LLP, Chicago, Amy Hawkinson

Skidmore, Owings & Merrill LLP, New York, Lauren Bebry and Elizabeth Kubany

Taipei Architects Association, Taipei

TRHY - TR Hamzah & Yeang Sdn Bhd, Ampang, Anderson Lee